For the Love of cupcakes

Publisher's Note: Raw or semi-cooked eggs should not be consumed by babies, toddlers, pregnant or breastfeeding women, the elderly or those suffering from a chronic illness.

Publisher & Creative Director: Nick Wells
Senior Project Editor: Catherine Taylor
Photography: Colin Bowling
Home economist and stylist: Ann Nicol
Copy Editor: Constance Novis
Art Director: Mike Spender
Layout Design: Jane Ashley
Digital Design & Production: Chris Herbert

Special thanks to Digby Smith and Helen Wall, and to the following for supplying materials for photography:

For all cake-decorating supplies by mail order, such as paper cases, sugarpaste, fondant, icing colours and equipment and bakeware: Squires Group, Squires House, 3 Waverley Lane, Farnham, Surrey, GU9 8BB. Tel: 0845 22 55 67 1/2. www.squires-shop.com

For bakeware, muffin trays and paper cases by mail order:
Lakeland, Alexandria Buildings, Windermere, Cumbria, LA23 1BQ. Tel: 01539 488 100. www.lakeland.co.uk

This is a FLAME TREE book

FLAME TREE PUBLISHING
Crabtree Hall, Crabtree Lane
Fulham, London SW6 6TY
United Kingdom
www.flametreepublishing.com

Flame Tree is part of The Foundry Creative Media Company Limited

First published 2011

Copyright © 2011 Flame Tree Publishing

11 13 15 14 12
1 3 5 7 9 10 8 6 4 2

ISBN: 978-1-84786-977-7

Printed in China

For the Love of
cupcakes

Ann Nicol

**FLAME TREE
PUBLISHING**

For the Love of Cupcakes

Contents

Introduction

Why are cupcakes so popular? They seem to be on sale everywhere these days, but, as these little cakes are so quick and easy (you will find that most of the recipes in this book take under half an hour to bake), it is so simple to make your own. Cupcakes are delightful and versatile – ideal for an informal tea, a special occasion or for children's parties.

There is no comparison to the quality of home-made cakes and the fun to be had in making and baking them, and, as shop-bought cakes are expensive, you will notice the difference in price too. You also have plenty of scope for decorating, so you can create tailor-made treats for all sorts of occasions.

As a gift or a centrepiece, a batch of cupcakes brings a personal touch to any celebration, from a wedding anniversary to a children's party. This book has cakes for every occasion, some very quick and easy, some requiring a little more patience. If you are short on time, I have included tips on preparing ahead and freezing to make life easy.

Baking is a good way to introduce children to the art of cookery and these recipes will help to teach the basic techniques. Children also love the decorating part, and there are lots of ideas here to choose from.

So what is the best part of baking cupcakes? Well, they give so much pleasure: you get a real sense of satisfaction when you create a fresh batch of delicious cakes, accompanied by the marvellous aroma of baking that fills your home; and just watch the delighted reaction when you give them to your friends and neighbours.

How to Use This Book

This book is aimed at both those new to baking and experienced bakers, and shows how to create these popular mini-cakes, from the right equipment and ingredients to the cake and its decoration.

Just follow our simple step-by-step guides to ensure successful results. The choice is yours – you can make large, deep cakes, standard cupcakes and delicate small cupcakes, or even mini cupcakes. The size of each cake will depend on the depth of your trays and how deeply you fill the paper cases.

This book is divided into sections that deal with different types of cakes, including family favourites and fairy cakes for teatime treats, luscious chocolate cakes, and small cakes decorated for special occasions such as birthdays, Mother's Day, weddings and Christmas.

Baking and cake decoration involve many different techniques and a little skill is needed for certain cakes, but you will build up your confidence through practice. To help you achieve success every time, there are tips on choosing the right type of muffin and bun trays and paper liners. Using the very best ingredients is important, as are utensils

and careful weighing and measuring. You will not achieve good results without first checking your oven for correct temperatures and exact timings (*see* below).

Check Your Oven

Each recipe begins with an oven setting, and it is important to preheat the oven to the correct temperature before placing the cupcakes in to bake. As well as preheating the oven, it is important to arrange the shelves in the correct position in the oven before you start. The best baking position for cupcakes is just above the centre of the oven and best results are achieved by baking only one tray at a time. If you bake two trays at once, you may find the lower tray will come out with flatter tops to the cakes.

Many of us have fan-assisted ovens. These circulate hot air round the oven and heat up very quickly. For fan ovens, you will need to reduce the temperature stated in the recipe by 10 per cent, which is usually 20°C. For example, if the stated temperature in a recipe is 180°C, reduce it to 160°C for a fan-assisted oven. However, ovens do vary, so follow your manufacturer's instructions and get to know the way your oven heats. If your oven is too hot, the outsides of the cakes will burn before the interior has had time to cook. If it is too cool, the cakes may sink or not rise evenly. Try not to open the oven door until at least halfway through the baking time, when the cakes have had time to rise and set, as a sudden drop in temperature will stop the cakes rising and they may sink.

Measuring

All of the recipes in this book give metric and imperial measurements, but you must stick to one set only, as they are not exact equivalents. All spoon measurements should be used level for accuracy, and always use a recognized set of metric or imperial spoon measures for best results. Do not use domestic teaspoons and tablespoons as measures, as these may be deeper or shallower than a proper measuring spoon. Never estimate weights, as you will not achieve an accurate result. Good kitchen scales are a vital piece of equipment. Old-fashioned scales with a pan and a set of weights or modern ones with a digital display screen are equally good, as long as they are accurate. A measuring jug marked with small measures for smaller amounts is vital for liquids.

Equipment and Utensils

Bakeware

Metal Muffin Trays

Muffin trays come in different sizes. The standard-size tray has 12 holes, about 3 cm/1¼ inches deep, but they are also available with six deeper-set holes or with shallower indentations (often known as 'bun trays' or 'fairy-cake trays'), for making smaller cupcakes, or even with 'mini' holes (see right).

When purchasing, buy the heaviest tray you can afford – although these will be expensive, they produce the best results because they distribute the heat well and do not buckle.

If using trays without a nonstick finish, it is advisable to give these a light greasing before use. To grease trays, apply a thin film of melted vegetable margarine with a pastry brush or rub round the tray with kitchen paper and a little softened butter or margarine. You will normally need to line metal muffin trays with deep paper muffin cases or strips of baking parchment.

Mini-muffin Trays

These have small individual holes that can be half the diameter of holes in the bigger muffin trays, and as shallow as 1.75 cm/¾ inch deep. They can be made of metal, but the silicone pans are particularly useful for mini muffins because they turn out so easily and give a good shape.

Silicone Muffin Trays and Cupcake Cases

These are flexible and produce very good results. Although they are sold as nonstick, it is still advisable to rub round the inside of each hole or case with a little oil on some kitchen paper to prevent sticking. Individual silicone cupcake cases

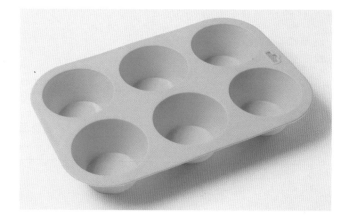

come in many bright colours and, unlike paper cases, are reusable. Simply wash out any crumbs after use in soapy water and leave them to dry, or clean them in the dishwasher.

Paper Cases

These come in many varieties, colours and shapes. It is advisable to buy the more expensive types, which are thicker and give a good shape to the cake as it rises. Oil and moisture is less likely to penetrate the thicker cases, whereas it may show through the cheaper ones. Metallic

gold, silver and coloured cupcake cases give good results and create a stunning effect for a special occasion. Cupcake cases also come in mini-muffin sizes. These may not be so easy to find but can be bought from mail-order cake decoration suppliers.

Baking Papers and Foil

Nonstick baking parchment is useful for lining the bases of trays and tins or for drying out chocolate and sugarpaste shapes. It is generally more versatile than greaseproof paper. However, greaseproof paper is useful for making triangular paper icing bags. Baking parchment can be used, but greaseproof paper is better, as it is thinner and more flexible. A large sheet of kitchen foil is handy for wrapping cakes or for protecting wrapped cakes in the freezer.

Electric Mixers

A hand-held electric mixer makes quick work of whisking butter and sugar and is an invaluable aid for baking, while a large tabletop mixer is useful if you are making larger quantities of cakes and frostings. Do not be tempted to use a food processor for mixing small amounts, as it is easy to over-process and this may produce flat cakes.

Other Essential Items

In addition to the usual variety of mixing bowls, wooden spoons, measuring spoons, scissors, sieves, graters, skewers for testing cakes and wire racks for cooling, the following are particularly useful in cupcake-making.

Pastry Brush

A pastry brush is used for brushing glazes over cakes and melted butter round tins. As brushes tend to wear out regularly and shed their bristles, keep a spare new brush to hand.

Palette Knives

A small and a large flat palette knife are ideal for many jobs, including loosening cakes from their tins, lifting cakes and swirling on buttercream icing. A palette knife with a cranked blade is useful for lifting small cakes or flat pieces of sugarpaste.

Stamps and Cutters

Stamps and cutters in almost any imaginable shape can be bought from specialist cake and baking stores. They come in classic metal cookie-cutter styles, in plastic, or as plunger-style. If you do not have appropriate cutters, you can use images found in books or magazines as templates.

Decorating Bags and Decorating Sets

A nylon decorating or 'piping' bag that comes with a set of five nozzles is a very useful piece of equipment for decorating

with icings. Look for a set with a plain nozzle and various star nozzles for piping swirls round cupcakes. The larger the star nozzle, the wider the swirls will be on the finished cake. Disposable paper or clear plastic icing bags are available, but nylon piping bags can be washed out in warm soapy water and dried out, ready to re-use again and again.

To Make a Paper Icing Bag

Cut out a 38 x 25.5 cm/15 x 10 inch rectangle of greaseproof paper. Fold it diagonally in half to form two triangular shapes. Cut along the fold line to make two triangles. One of these triangles can be used another time – it is quicker and easier to make two at a time from one square than to measure and mark out a triangle on a sheet of paper.

Fold one of the points on the long side of the triangle over the top to make a sharp cone and hold in the centre. Fold the other sharp end of the triangle over the cone. Hold all the points together at the back of the cone, keeping the pointed end sharp. Turn the points inside the top edge, fold over to make a crease, then secure with a piece of sticky tape. To use, snip away the end, place a piping nozzle in position and fill the bag with icing, or fill the bag with icing first, then snip away a tiny hole at the end for piping a plain edge, writing or piping tiny dots.

Ingredients

In cupcake-making, the classic cake base is made in the same way as any typical cake – that is, by mixing fats, sugar, flour and eggs together and varying with further ingredients or different methods to achieve the required result. Here is a selected outline of ingredients that are particularly useful or important in cupcake-making – which is mainly in the area of decorating!

Remember that when a recipe calls for 'softened' butter or margarine, it means *block* butter or margarine that has been removed from the refrigerator a little while before required – they are much easier to mix in when at room temperature.

Yogurt and Buttermilk

Plain yogurt is great for adding to sweet and savoury muffins, as it adds richness and moisture to smaller cakes. Do not use low-fat yogurt – stick to plain, thickset natural yogurts that have more substance to them.

Buttermilk is produced by adding bacteria to low-fat milk to thicken and sour it. This is used in recipes that use bicarbonate of soda, as the acidity from the buttermilk produces carbon dioxide, which raises the cakes. Buttermilk will give an extra lift to cupcakes, as well as a richer flavour. You will find buttermilk on sale in the dairy section of larger supermarkets but, if it is not available, use 1 tbsp lemon juice to 300 ml/½ pint plain yogurt or whole milk as a substitute.

Extracts

Flavouring extracts are very concentrated and usually sold in liquid form in small bottles. A teaspoon measure will usually be enough to flavour a cake mixture for 12 muffins. Vanilla and almond extracts are ideal to impart their delicate flavours into cake mixtures and you will find the more expensive extracts give a finer and more natural flavour. Rosewater can be used for flavouring both cake mixtures and icings and has a delicate, perfumed flavour. Fruit flavourings, such as lemon, lime, orange and raspberry, will give a fresh twist to mixtures and icings.

Chocolate

For the best results and a professional finish and flavour, it is always advisable to buy the highest quality chocolate you can find, although this will be more expensive. Better-quality chocolates contain a higher percentage of real cocoa fat, which gives a flavour and texture far superior to cheaper varieties. (Cheaper chocolate labelled as 'cooking' or 'baking' chocolate contains a much smaller percentage of cocoa solids and is best avoided in favour of better-quality eating chocolate.) Chocoalte marked as 70-per-cent cocoa solids will give the best results and you will find this chocolate is shiny and brittle and it should snap very easily.

Dark Chocolate

Also known as 'plain' or 'plain dark' chocolate, this is the most useful all-purpose type of chocolate for baking, as it has a good strong flavour.

Milk Chocolate

Milk chocolate has sugar added and is sweeter than dark, so is good for melting for icings and decorations.

White Chocolate

This is not strictly chocolate, as it contains only cocoa butter, milk and sugar. It is expensive and the most difficult to work with, so must be used with care. It is best to grate it finely and keep the temperature very low when melting it.

Chocolate Cake Covering

This is a cheaper substitute containing a minimum of 2.5-per-cent cocoa solids and vegetable oil. It is considerably cheaper than real chocolate and the flavour is not as good, but it is easy to melt and sets quickly and well for a coating.

Chocolate Chips

Chips come in dark, milk and white varieties and are sold in small bags. They are useful for adding to cupcake and muffin mixtures to enrich them and add a delicious texture as they part melt into the cakes on baking.

Cocoa Powder

Cocoa powder needs to be cooked to release the full flavour, so blend it with boiling water to make into a paste, then cool, before adding to a recipe, or sift it into the bowl with the flour.

Drinking Chocolate

Be aware that this is not the same as cocoa, as it contains milk powder and sugar. Some recipes may specify using drinking chocolate and these are successful, but do not substitute it for cocoa powder, as it will spoil the flavour of a cake.

For Decorating

Icing Sugar

Icing sugar is fine and powdery. It is usually sold plain and white, but can also be bought as an unrefined golden (or 'natural') variety. Use it for delicate icings, frostings and decorations. Store this sugar in a dry place, as it can absorb moisture and this will make it go hard and lumpy. Always sift this sugar at least once, or preferably twice, before you use it, to remove any hard lumps that would prevent icing from achieving a smooth texture – lumpy icing is impossible to pipe out.

Fondant Icing Sugar

This is sold in plain and flavoured varieties and gives a beautiful glossy finish to cake toppings. Just add a little boiled water to the sugar, according to the packet instructions, to make a shiny icing that can be poured or drizzled over cupcake tops to give a very professional finish. Colour the plain white icing with a few spots of paste food colour to achieve your desired result.

Flavoured fondant icing sugar is sold in strawberry, raspberry, orange, lemon and blackcurrant flavours and also has colouring added. These sugars are ideal if you want to make a large batch of cakes with different coloured and flavoured toppings. Flavoured fondant icing sugars can also be whisked with softened unsalted butter and cream cheese to make delicious frostings in just a few moments.

Royal Icing Sugar

Royal icing sets to a classic, firm Christmas-cake-style covering. This ready-mixed sugar is whisked with cold water to give an instant royal icing. It has dried egg white included in the mixture, so does not need the long beating that traditional royal icing recipes require. It is also ideal to use for those who cannot eat raw egg whites.

Tubes of Writing Icing

You can buy small tubes of coloured royal icing or gel icing, usually in sets of black, red, yellow and blue, and these are ideal for small amounts of writing or for piping on dots or small decorations.

Food Colourings

You can buy food colourings in liquid, paste, gel and powder or dust forms in a great range of colours.

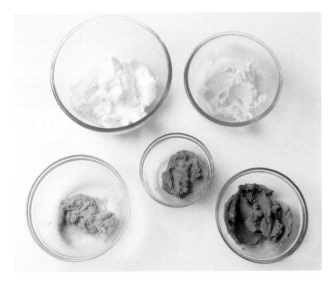

Dusts and sparkle colourings These should be lightly brushed onto dry sugarpaste to form a delicate sheen to decorations such as flowers.

Bought Sugar Decorations and Sprinkles

A selection of pretty sprinkles can be bought in supermarkets or by mail order from specialist cake decorating companies, and these provide a wonderful way to make quick and easy cake toppings.

Paste food colourings These are best for using with sugarpaste. They are sold in small tubs and are very concentrated, so should be added to the sugarpaste dot by dot on the end of a cocktail stick. Knead the colouring in evenly, adding more until you get the colour you require.

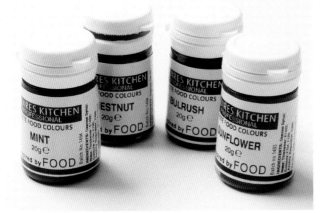

Liquid and gel food colourings Gel colourings are ideal for adding to frostings. Add this cautiously, drop by drop, beating the frosting well until you reach the colour you require.

Basic Methods

Different Mixing Techniques

Creaming

The creaming method – which means that the butter and sugar are first beaten or 'creamed' together – makes light cakes. A little care is needed for this method. Use a large mixing bowl to beat the fat and sugar together until pale and fluffy. The eggs are gradually beaten in to form a slackened batter and the flour is folded in last, to stiffen up the mixture.

Rubbing In

In this method, the fat is lightly worked into the flour between the fingers, as in pastry-making, until the

mixture resembles fine crumbs. This can be done by hand or in a food processor. Enough liquid is stirred in to give a soft mixture that will drop easily from a spoon. This method is used for easy fruit cakes and small buns such as rock cakes.

All-In-One Mixtures

This 'one stage' method is quick and easy and is perfect for those new to baking, as it does not involve any complicated techniques. It is ideal for making light sponges, but soft tub-type margarine or softened butter at room temperature must

be used. All the ingredients are simply placed in a large bowl and quickly beaten together for just a few minutes until smooth. Be careful not to overbeat, as this will make the mixture too wet. Self-raising flour with the addition of a little extra baking powder is vital for a good rise.

The Melting Method

Cakes with a delicious moist, sticky texture, such as gingerbread, are made by this method. These cakes use a high proportion of sugar and syrup, which are gently

warmed together in a saucepan with the fat, until the sugar has dissolved and the mixture is liquid. It is important to cool the hot melted mixture a little before beating in flour, eggs and spices to make the batter, otherwise it will damage the power of the raising agent.

Checking to See if the Cakes Are Cooked

Small cupcakes and muffins should be golden, risen and firm to the touch when pressed lightly in the centre. The last part of a cupcake or muffin to cook is the centre, so, after the baking time stated, check this area. For light sponge-type cakes, press the centre lightly with the fingertips and, if the cake is cooked, it should spring back easily. To test more

thoroughly, insert a thin warmed skewer into the deepest part of the centre. If the cake is cooked, it will come out perfectly clean with no mixture sticking to it, but, if there is some on the skewer, bake the cakes for a little longer and test again.

Cooling the Cakes

All freshly baked cakes are very fragile; they need to stand in the tins to cool for a short time to make them firm. Sponges and delicate cupcakes need standing time of about 2 minutes, muffins need 3–4 minutes and fruity mixtures need 5 minutes.

If muffins start to stick to their moulds, leave until the cakes are firm, then loosen their sides by running round the trays with a small palette knife. Carefully turn the cakes out on a wire rack to cool. Do not leave cupcakes in paper cases in the bun trays to cool completely, as moisture that collects in the bun trays will cause the paper cases to go damp and discolour.

How to Patch Up Mistakes

- If your cakes have peaked, trim them flat when the cakes are cold (*see* right).

- If the cakes have overcooked or are burnt on the outside, simply scrape this away with a serrated knife and cover the surface with buttercream.

- If the cakes are a little dry, sprinkle them with a few drops of sweet sherry or orange juice.

Cutting the Tops Level

Many cupcakes will form a small peak while baking and this is an ideal shape for coating with buttercream or piping round a swirl of cream cheese icing. However, some methods of decorating cakes require a flat surface, so, for these, trim the tops level with a sharp knife. Coat the cakes with apricot glaze and press on a disc of almond paste or sugarpaste to give you a flat surface to decorate.

Storing Cupcakes

- Make sure cakes are completely cold before storing, otherwise condensation can form in the container and this can cause the cakes to go mouldy.

- Large, shallow plastic food containers with airtight lids are ideal for cupcakes and muffins, as they enable the cakes to be kept flat in one single layer and even small cupcakes will stay moist. Old-fashioned cake tins can be used, but they do not hold a large number of small cakes. If you do not have a cake tin or container that is big enough, invert a large mixing bowl over the cupcakes on a plate or flat surface and this will keep them fresh.

- Sponge cakes will keep for 3–4 days, and richer fruit cakes for 5 days to a week. Cakes with fresh cream fillings and decorations need to be kept in the refrigerator and are best eaten on the day of filling with cream.

- Store cakes with sugarpaste decorations in a cool place, but *not* in the refrigerator. The moisture in a refrigerator will be absorbed by the sugarpaste and the icing will go limp and soggy.

Freezing Cupcakes

Most cupcakes will freeze well, but, for best results, freeze undecorated. Completely cool each cake and freeze in one layer on a baking sheet or flat tray. Once frozen, place in strong freezer bags or boxes and seal to exclude as much air as possible, label and freeze. Cakes containing fresh fruits such as blueberries or raspberries will not freeze well, as the fruit tends to make the cakes soggy when thawed, so these are best eaten fresh on the day of baking.

To use frozen cakes, completely unwrap and thaw at room temperature on racks. The paper cases may peel away from frozen cakes, so these may need to be replaced with fresh ones before decorating the cakes.

Basic Cake Recipes

Basic Vanilla Cupcakes

**Makes 18 deep cupcakes, 24 fairy cakes or
36 mini cupcakes**

225 g/8 oz butter, softened
225 g/8 oz caster sugar
4 medium eggs, beaten
225 g/8 oz self-raising flour
½ tsp baking powder
2 tbsp semi-skimmed milk
1 tsp vanilla extract
1 tsp glycerine

Preheat the oven to 180°C/350°F/Gas Mark 4 and line
appropriate trays with enough paper cases. Whisk the butter
and sugar together, preferably with an electric hand mixer,
until pale and fluffy. Whisk in the eggs gradually, adding a
teaspoon of flour with each addition to prevent the mixture
from curdling.

Sift the remaining flour and baking powder into the bowl,
then gradually whisk in the milk, extract and glycerine. Spoon
the mixture into the paper cases and bake for 25 minutes for
the larger cakes, 15 minutes for the fairy cakes or 12 minutes
for the mini cupcakes, or until firm and golden. Cool on a
wire rack. Keep for 3–4 days in an airtight container.

Mini Cupcakes

Makes about 24

100 g/3½ oz golden caster sugar
100 g/3½ oz butter, softened

finely grated zest and juice of ½ lemon
2 medium eggs, beaten
100 g/3½ oz self-raising flour
2 tsp milk

Preheat the oven to 190°C/375°F/Gas Mark 5. Grease a
mini-muffin tray or line it with mini paper cases. Put the
sugar, butter and lemon zest in a large bowl and beat until
light and fluffy. Add the beaten eggs a little at a time,
adding a teaspoon of flour with each addition. Fold in the
remaining flour, lemon juice and milk and mix until smooth.

Spoon into the mini-muffin tray or cases and bake for about
12 minutes until golden and risen. Transfer to a wire rack to
cool. Keep for 2–3 days in an airtight container.

225 g/8 oz self-raising flour
1 tsp ground mixed spice
finely grated zest, and 1 tbsp juice, of 1 orange
1 tbsp black treacle
350 g/12 oz mixed dried fruit

Preheat the oven to 180°C/350°F/Gas Mark 4. Line two bun trays with 18 paper fairy-cake cases. Beat the butter and sugar together until light and fluffy, then beat in the eggs a little at a time, adding a teaspoon of flour with each addition. Sift in the remaining flour and spice, add the orange zest and juice, treacle and dried fruit to the bowl and fold together until the mixture is blended.

Spoon into the cases and bake for 30 minutes until firm in the centre and a skewer comes out clean. Leave to cool in the trays for 15 minutes, then turn out to cool on a wire rack. Store in an airtight container for up to 4 weeks, or freeze until needed.

Quick All-in-One Mix for Cupcakes

Makes 12 deep cupcakes or 18 fairy cakes

125 g/4 oz caster sugar
125 g/4 oz soft tub margarine
2 medium eggs
125 g/4 oz self-raising flour
1 tsp milk or lemon juice

Preheat the oven to 190°C/375°F/Gas Mark 5. Line appropriate trays with enough paper cases for the cakes. Place all the cake ingredients in a large bowl and beat with an electric mixer for about 2 minutes until smooth. Half-fill the paper cases with the mixture. Bake for about 15 minutes until firm, risen and golden. Remove to a wire rack to cool. Keep for 2–3 days in an airtight container.

Individual Fruitcakes

Makes 18 fairy cakes

125 g/4 oz butter
125 g/4 oz soft dark muscovado sugar
2 medium eggs, beaten

Chocolate Fudge Cupcakes

**Makes 12 deep cupcakes, 18 cupcakes or
22 mini cupcakes**

150 g/5 oz butter, softened

150 g/5 oz golden caster sugar

3 medium eggs, beaten

125 g/4 oz self-raising flour

25 g/1 oz cocoa powder

1 tbsp milk

Preheat the oven to 190°C/375°F/Gas Mark 5. Line
appropriate trays with enough foil or paper cases. Place the
butter, caster sugar and eggs in a large bowl and then sift in
the flour and cocoa powder. Whisk together with the milk
until smooth for about 2 minutes, then spoon into the cases,
filling them two-thirds full.

Bake for about 20 minutes for the deep cakes, 14 minutes
for the cupcakes or 12–14 minutes for the mini cupcakes
until well risen and springy to the touch. Cool on a wire
rack. Keep for 3 days in an airtight container.

Carrot Cupcakes

**Makes 12 deep cupcakes, 18 cupcakes or
22 mini cupcakes**

225 g/8 oz carrots, peeled

175 g/6 oz self-raising wholemeal flour

1 tsp baking powder

½ tsp ground cinnamon

pinch salt

150 ml/¼ pt sunflower oil

150 g/5 oz soft light brown sugar

3 medium eggs, beaten

1 tsp vanilla extract

50 g/2 oz sultanas or raisins

Preheat the oven to 180°C/350°F/Gas Mark 4. Lightly oil
or line appropriate trays with enough paper cases. Grate the
carrots finely. Sift the flour, baking powder, cinnamon and
salt into a bowl, then tip in any bran from the sieve. Add the
oil, sugar, eggs, extract, sultanas and grated carrots.

Beat until smooth, then spoon into the prepared trays or
cases. Bake for 25 minutes for the deep cupcakes, 20
minutes for the cupcakes or 15–20 minutes for the mini
cupcakes until risen and golden. Cool on a wire rack. Keep
for up to 5 days in an airtight container.

Basic Icing Recipes

Cream Cheese Frosting

Covers 12 cupcakes

50 g/2 oz unsalted butter, softened
300 g/11 oz icing sugar, sifted
flavouring of choice
food colourings of choice
125 g/4 oz full-fat cream cheese

Beat the butter and icing sugar together until light and
fluffy. Add flavourings and colourings of choice and beat
again. Add the cream cheese and whisk until light and
fluffy. Do not overbeat, however, as the mixture can
become runny.

Basic Buttercream Frosting

Covers 12 cupcakes

150 g/5 oz unsalted butter, softened
225 g/8 oz icing sugar, sifted
2 tbsp hot milk or water
1 tsp vanilla extract
food colourings of choice

Beat the butter until light and fluffy, then beat in half the
sifted icing sugar and half the hot milk or water, then beat in
the remaining icing sugar and milk or water. Add the vanilla
extract and any food colourings. Store chilled for up to
2 days in a lidded container.

Chocolate Fudge Icing

Covers 12 cupcakes

125 g/4 oz dark chocolate, broken into pieces
50 g/2 oz unsalted butter

whisk in the egg with the icing sugar and vanilla extract. Whisk until smooth and glossy, then use immediately, or leave to cool and thicken for a spreading consistency.

Royal Icing

Makes 450 g/1 lb (enough to cover 12 deep cupcakes)

2 medium egg whites
500 g/1 lb 2 oz icing sugar, sifted
2 tsp lemon juice

Put the egg whites in a large bowl and whisk lightly with a fork until foamy. Sift in half the icing sugar with the lemon juice and beat well with an electric mixer for 4 minutes, or by hand with a wooden spoon for about 10 minutes, until smooth.

Gradually sift in the remaining icing sugar and beat again until thick, smooth and brilliant white and the icing

1 medium egg, beaten
175 g/6 oz natural icing sugar, sifted
½ tsp vanilla extract

Place the chocolate and butter in a bowl over a pan of hot water and stir until melted. Remove from the heat and

forms soft peaks when flicked up with a spoon. Keep the royal icing covered with a clean damp cloth until you are ready to use it, or store in the refrigerator in a tightly lidded plastic container until needed. If making royal icing ahead of time to use later, beat it again before use to remove any air bubbles that may have formed in the mixture.

Tip For a softer royal icing that will not set too hard, beat 1 tsp glycerine into the mixture.

Glacé Icing

Covers 12 cupcakes

225 g/8 oz icing sugar
few drops lemon juice or vanilla or almond extract
2–3 tbsp boiling water
liquid food colouring (optional)

Sift the icing sugar into a bowl and add the chosen flavouring. Gradually stir in enough water to mix to a consistency of thick cream. Beat with a wooden spoon until the icing is thick enough to coat the back of the spoon. Add colouring, if liked, and use at once, as the icing will begin to form a skin.

Apricot Glaze

Makes 450 g/1 lb to cover 24 cupcakes

450 g/1 lb apricot jam
3 tbsp water
1 tsp lemon juice

Place the jam, water and juice in a heavy-based saucepan and heat gently, stirring, until soft and melted. Boil rapidly for 1 minute, then press through a fine sieve with the back of a wooden spoon. Discard the pieces of fruit. Use immediately for glazing or sticking on almond paste, or pour into a clean jar or plastic lidded container and refrigerate for up to 3 months.

Almond Paste

Makes 450 g/1 lb to cover 24 cupcakes

125 g/4 oz sifted icing sugar
125 g/4 oz caster sugar
225 g/8 oz ground almonds
1 medium egg
1 tsp lemon juice

Stir the sugars and ground almonds together in a bowl. Whisk the egg and lemon juice together and mix into the dry ingredients.

Knead until the paste is smooth. Wrap tightly in clingfilm or foil to keep airtight and store in the refrigerator until needed. The paste can be made 2–3 days ahead of time, but after that it will start to dry out and become difficult to handle.

To use the almond paste, knead on a surface lightly dusted with icing sugar until soft and pliable. Brush the top of each cake with apricot glaze. Roll out the almond paste and cut out discs large enough to cover the tops of the cakes. Press onto the cakes.

Ready-to-roll Fondant Icing

(Sugarpaste Icing)
Makes 350 g/12 oz (or enough cover 12 cupcakes)

1 medium egg white
1 tbsp liquid glucose
350 g/12 oz icing sugar, sifted

Place the egg white and liquid glucose in a large mixing bowl and stir together with a fork, breaking up the egg white. Add the icing sugar gradually, mixing in with a palette knife until the mixture binds together and forms a ball. Turn the ball of icing out onto a clean surface dusted with icing sugar and knead for 5 minutes until soft but firm enough to roll out. If the icing is too soft, knead in a little more icing sugar until the mixture is pliable.

To colour, knead in paste food colouring. Do not use liquid food colourings, as this is not suitable and will make the sugarpaste go limp.

To use, roll out thinly on a clean surface dusted with icing sugar and cut out discs large enough to cover the top of each cake. Brush the almond paste (if using as a layer underneath the sugarpaste discs) with a little cold boiled water or a clear spirit such as kirsch and press onto the cake, then press the sugarpaste on top of the almond paste topping. Alternatively, coat the cakes with a little buttercream, place the sugarpaste disc on top and press down.

To mould, knead lightly and roll out thinly on a surface dusted with icing sugar. Use cutters or templates to make flat flowers or shapes (*see* Making Flat Decorations, pages 37–38). Mould into 3D shapes with your fingertips and leave to dry out for 24 hours in egg boxes lined with clingfilm.

Decorating Techniques and Tips

Using Chocolate

Melting Chocolate

Care and attention is needed to melt chocolate for baking
and cake decorating needs. If the chocolate gets too hot or
comes into contact with water or steam, it will 'seize' or
stiffen and form into a hard ball instead of a smooth melted
mixture. You can add a little vegetable oil or margarine, a
teaspoon at a time, to the mixture to make it liquid again.

To melt chocolate, break the bar into small pieces, or grate
or chop it, and place in a heatproof bowl standing over a
bowl of warm, not hot, water. Make sure the bowl
containing the chocolate is completely dry and that steam or
water cannot enter the bowl. Heat the water to a gentle
simmer only and leave the bowl to stand for about 5
minutes. Do not let the water get too hot or the chocolate
will reach too high a temperature and will lose its sheen.

The microwave oven is ideal for melting chocolate. Place the
chocolate pieces in a small microwave-proof bowl and melt
gently on low or defrost settings in small bursts of 30
seconds, checking and stirring in between, until the
chocolate has melted.

Making Chocolate Decorations

Curls and shavings Spread melted chocolate out thinly
onto a clean dry surface such as a plastic board, marble or a
clean worktop. Leave the chocolate until almost set, then
pull a long sharp-bladed knife through it at an angle to form
curls or shavings. Place the curls in a lidded plastic box in the
refrigerator until needed for decoration.

Leaves Wash and dry holly or rose leaves and place on a
sheet of nonstick baking parchment. Melt the chocolate and
paint on the underside of each leaf. Leave to dry out, then

carefully peel away the leaf. You will find the veined side is uppermost on the chocolate leaf. Place in a lidded container and keep refrigerated until needed for decoration.

Crystallizing Petals, Flowers, Leaves, and Berries

Wash and dry herbs and leaves such as rosemary sprigs and small bay leaves or berries such as cranberries. Separate edible petals from small flowers such as rosebuds and clean small flowers such as violets with a clean brush, but do not wash them.

Beat 1 medium egg white with 2 tsp cold water until frothy. Paint a thin layer of egg white carefully over the items, then sprinkle lightly with caster sugar, shaking to remove any excess. Leave to dry on a wire rack lined with nonstick baking parchment.

Using Buttercream and Cream Cheese Frostings

These soft icings can be swirled onto the tops of cupcakes with a small palette knife or placed in a piping bag fitted with a star nozzle to pipe impressive whirls.

- Do not be mean with the amount of frosting you use. If this is scraped on thinly, you will see the cake underneath, so be generous.

- Keep cupcakes with frostings in a cool place, or refrigerate, as they contain a high percentage of butter, which will melt easily in too warm a place.

- Cupcakes coated in buttercream can be decorated easily with colourful sprinkles and coarse coloured sugars. To make this easy, place the sprinkles in a small saucer or on a piece of nonstick baking parchment and roll the outside edges of each cupcake in the decorations.

Using Ready-to-roll Fondant

Fondant (sugarpaste) is a versatile icing, as it can be used for covering cupcakes or modelling all sorts of fancy decorations. To use as a covering, roll out the sugarpaste thinly on a surface dusted with icing sugar and cut out circles the size of the cake tops. Coat each cake with a little apricot glaze or buttercream and press on the circles to form a flat surface.

Making Flat Decorations

To make letters, numbers or flat decorations, roll out the sugarpaste thinly and cut out the shapes freehand or with

Decorating Tips

- Always roll out almond paste or sugarpaste on a surface lightly dusted with icing sugar.

- Leave sugarpaste-covered cakes to firm up for 2 hours before adding decorations, as this provides a good finished surface to work on.

- Tie ribbons round the finished cake and secure them with a dab of royal icing. Never use pins in ribbons on a cake.

- Once decorated, store sugarpaste-covered cakes in large boxes in a cool place. Do not store in a refrigerator, as the sugarpaste will become damp and colours may run.

- Paste food colourings are best for working with sugarpaste and a little goes a very long way. As these are very concentrated, use a cocktail stick to add dots of paste gradually, until you are sure of the colour, and knead in until even.

cutters. You may have some templates or images that you would like to replicate, in which case, trace the pattern you want onto a sheet of clear greaseproof paper or nonstick baking parchment, then position the paper over the sugarpaste. Mark over the pattern with the tip of a small sharp knife or a pin. Remove the paper and cut out the marked-on pattern with a small sharp knife. Leave your shapes to dry on nonstick baking parchment on a flat surface or a tray for 2–3 hours to make them firm and easy to handle.

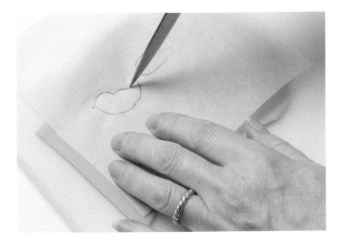

Delectable
Delights

Mini Carrot Cupcakes

Makes 22

175 g/6 oz self-raising wholemeal flour
1 tsp baking powder
½ tsp ground cinnamon
pinch salt
150 ml/¼ pint sunflower oil
150 g/5 oz soft light brown sugar
3 medium eggs, beaten
1 tsp vanilla extract
50 g/2 oz sultanas
225 g/8 oz carrots, peeled and grated

To decorate:
1 orange
75 g/3 oz cream cheese
175 g/6 oz golden icing sugar

1. Preheat the oven to 180°C/350°F/Gas Mark 4. Lightly oil two 12-hole mini-muffin trays.

2. Sift the flour, baking powder, cinnamon and salt into a bowl, along with any bran from the sieve.

3. Add the oil, sugar, eggs, vanilla extract, sultanas and grated carrots. Beat until smooth, then spoon into the muffin trays. Bake for about 20 minutes until risen and golden. Cool on a wire rack.

4. To decorate, peel thin strips of zest from the orange. Beat the cream cheese and icing sugar together with 2 tsp juice from the orange to make a spreading consistency. Swirl the icing over each cupcake and then top with shreds of orange zest. Keep for up to 3 days in an airtight container in a cool place.

Shaggy Coconut Cupcakes

Makes 12

½ tsp baking powder
200 g/7 oz self-raising flour
175 g/6 oz caster sugar
2 tbsp desiccated coconut
175 g/6 oz soft tub margarine
3 medium eggs, beaten
2 tbsp milk

To decorate:
1 batch buttercream (*see* page 29)
1 tbsp coconut liqueur (optional)
175 g/6 oz large shredded coconut strands

1. Preheat the oven to 180°C/350°F/Gas Mark 4. Line a 12-hole deep muffin tray with paper cases.

2. Sift the baking powder and flour into a large bowl. Add all the remaining ingredients and beat for about 2 minutes until smooth and creamy. Divide evenly between the paper cases.

3. Bake for 18–20 minutes until risen, golden and firm to the touch. Leave in the muffin trays for 2 minutes, then turn out to cool on a wire rack.

4. To decorate the cupcakes, beat the coconut liqueur (if using) into the buttercream and then swirl the buttercream over each cupcake. Press large strands of shredded coconut into the buttercream. Keep for up to 3 days in an airtight container in a cool place.

Coffee & Walnut Fudge Cupcakes

Makes 16–18

125 g/4 oz self-raising flour
125 g/4 oz butter, softened
125 g/4 oz golden caster sugar
2 medium eggs, beaten
1 tbsp golden syrup
50 g/2 oz walnuts,
  finely chopped

To decorate:
225 g/8 oz golden
  icing sugar
125 g/4 oz unsalted butter,
  at room temperature
2 tsp coffee extract
16–18 small walnut pieces

1. Preheat the oven to 200°C/400°F/Gas Mark 6. Line two 12-hole bun trays with 16–18 small foil cases, depending on the depth of the tray holes.

2. Stir the flour into a bowl and add the butter, sugar, eggs and syrup. Beat for about 2 minutes, then fold in the walnuts.

3. Spoon the mixture into the paper cases and bake for about 12–14 minutes until well risen and springy in the centre. Remove to a wire rack to cool.

4. Make the frosting by sifting the icing sugar into a bowl. Add the butter, coffee extract and 1 tablespoon hot water. Beat until light and fluffy, then place in a piping bag fitted with a star nozzle. Pipe a swirl on each cupcake and top with a walnut piece. Keep for 3–4 days in an airtight container in a cool place.

Mini Cupcakes

Makes 24

100 g/3½ oz golden
  caster sugar
100 g/3½ oz butter, softened
finely grated zest of ½ lemon
  and 1 tsp juice
2 medium eggs, beaten
100 g/3½ oz self-raising flour

To decorate:
50 g/2 oz unsalted butter, softened
1 tsp vanilla extract
125 g/4 oz icing sugar, sifted
1 tbsp milk
paste food colourings
sugar sprinkles

1. Preheat the oven to 190°C/375°F/Gas Mark 5. Line a
   24-hole mini-muffin tray with paper mini-muffin cases.

2. Put the sugar, butter and lemon zest in a large bowl and
   beat until light and fluffy. Beat in the eggs a little at a
   time, adding a teaspoon of flour with each addition.
   Fold in the rest of the flour and the lemon juice and
   mix until smooth.

3. Spoon into the mini-muffin cases and bake for about
   12 minutes until golden and risen. Transfer to a wire
   rack to cool.

4. To make the icing, beat the butter and vanilla extract
   together until light and fluffy, then gradually beat in the
   icing sugar and milk until a soft, easy-to-spread
   consistency has formed. Colour the icing in batches with
   paste food colourings, then spread over the cold cupcakes
   with a flat-bladed knife. Decorate with sugar sprinkles.
   Keep in an airtight container for up to 2 days.

Banoffee Cupcakes

Makes 10–12

175 g/6 oz soft ripe bananas
125 g/4 oz soft tub margarine
75 g/3 oz golden caster sugar
1 tbsp milk
2 medium eggs
225 g/8 oz plain flour
1 tbsp baking powder
75 g/3 oz mini soft fudge pieces

To decorate:
125 g/4 oz golden
  icing sugar
10–12 semi-dried
  banana flakes

1. Preheat the oven to 180°C/350°F/Gas Mark 4. Line a
   12-hole muffin tray with 10–12 deep paper cases,
   depending on the depth of the holes.

2. Peel and mash the bananas in a large bowl, then add the
   margarine, sugar, milk and eggs. Sift in the flour and
   baking powder and beat together for about 2 minutes
   until smooth.

3. Fold in 50 g/2 oz of the fudge pieces and then spoon the
   mixture into the paper cases. Bake for about 20 minutes
   until golden and firm. Remove from the baking trays to a
   wire rack to cool.

4. For the decoration, blend the icing sugar with 3–4 tsp
   cold water to make a thin icing. Drizzle over the top of
   each cupcake and, while the icing is still wet, top with the
   remaining mini fudge pieces and the banana flakes. Leave
   to dry out for 30 minutes to set the icing. Keep in an
   airtight container for up to 3 days.

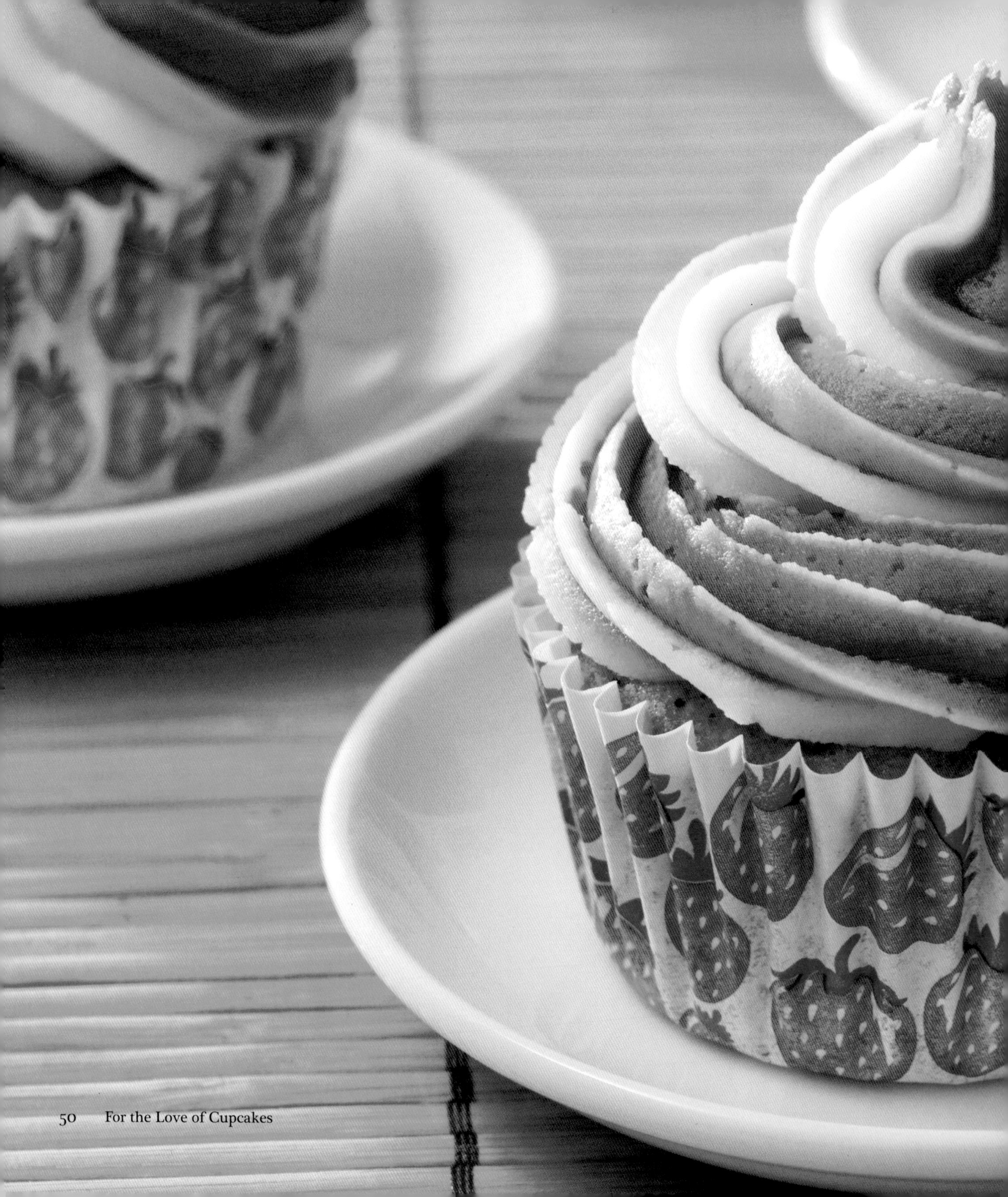

Strawberry Swirl Cupcakes

Makes 12

125 g/4 oz caster sugar
125 g/4 oz soft
  tub margarine
2 medium eggs
125 g/4 oz self-raising flour
½ tsp baking powder
2 tbsp sieved strawberry jam

To decorate:
50 g/2 oz unsalted butter
  at room temperature
300 g/11 oz icing
  sugar, sifted
125 g/4 oz full-fat
  cream cheese
1 tbsp sieved
  strawberry jam
pink food colouring

1. Preheat the oven to 190°C/375°F/Gas Mark 5. Line a muffin tray with 12 deep paper cases.

2. Place all the cupcake ingredients except the jam in a large bowl and beat with an electric mixer for about 2 minutes until smooth. Fill the paper cases halfway up with the mixture.

3. Add ½ tsp jam to each case and swirl it into the mixture. Bake for about 15 minutes until firm, risen and golden. Remove to a wire rack to cool.

4. To prepare the frosting, beat the butter until soft, then gradually add the icing sugar until the mixture is light. Add the cream cheese and whisk until light and fluffy.

5. Divide the mixture in half and beat the strawberry jam and pink food colouring into one half. Fit a piping bag with a wide star nozzle and spoon strawberry cream on one side of the bag and the plain cream on the other. Pipe swirls on top of the cupcakes. Keep for up to 3 days in an airtight container in a cool place.

Double Cherry Cupcakes

Makes 12

50 g/2 oz glacé cherries, washed,
  dried and chopped
125 g/4 oz self-raising flour
25 g/1 oz dried morello cherries
125 g/4 oz soft tub margarine
125 g/4 oz caster sugar
2 medium eggs
½ tsp almond extract

To decorate:
125 g/4 oz fondant
icing sugar
pale pink liquid food colouring
40 g/1½ oz glacé cherries

1. Preheat the oven to 190°C/375°F/Gas Mark 5. Line a 12-
   hole muffin tray with deep paper cases.

2. Dust the chopped glacé cherries lightly 1 tbsp of the flour,
   then mix with the morello cherries and set aside. Sift the
   rest of the flour into a bowl, then add the margarine, sugar,
   eggs and almond extract. Beat for about 2 minutes until
   smooth, then fold in the cherries.

3. Spoon the batter into the paper cases and bake for 15–20
   minutes until well risen and springy in the centre. Turn out
   to cool on a wire rack.

4. To decorate the cupcakes, trim the tops level. Mix the icing
   sugar with 2–3 tsp warm water and a few drops pink food
   colouring to make a thick consistency. Spoon the icing
   over each cupcake, filling right up to the edge.

5. Chop the cherries finely and sprinkle over the icing.
   Leave to set for 30 minutes. Keep for up to 3 days in an
   airtight container.

Ginger & Lemon
Cupcakes

Makes 18

8 tbsp golden syrup	**To decorate:**
125 g/4 oz block margarine	125 g/4 oz golden
225 g/8 oz plain flour	icing sugar
2 tsp ground ginger	1 tsp lemon juice
75 g/3 oz sultanas	glacé ginger pieces
50 g/2 oz soft dark	
brown sugar	
200 ml/7 fl oz milk	
1 tsp bicarbonate of soda	
1 medium egg, beaten	

1. Preheat the oven to 180°C/350°F/Gas Mark 4. Line two shallow muffin trays with 18 paper cases.

2. Place the syrup and margarine in a heavy-based pan and melt together gently. Sift the flour and ginger into a bowl, then stir in the sultanas and sugar. Warm the milk and stir in the bicarbonate of soda.

3. Pour the syrup mixture, milk and beaten egg into the dry ingredients and beat until smooth. Pour the mixture into a jug.

4. Carefully spoon 2 tbsp of the mixture into each case (the mixture will be wet). Bake for about 30 minutes. Cool in the trays for 10 minutes, then turn out to cool on a wire rack.

5. To decorate, blend the icing sugar with the lemon juice and 1 tbsp warm water to make a thin glacé icing. Drizzle over the top of each cupcake, then top with glacé ginger pieces. Leave to set for 30 minutes. Keep in an airtight container for up to 5 days.

Crystallized Violet Cupcakes

Makes 12

150 g/5 oz butter, softened
150 g/5 oz caster sugar
3 medium eggs, beaten
150 g/5 oz self-raising flour
½ tsp baking powder
1 lemon

To decorate:
12 fresh violets
1 egg white
caster sugar
125 g/4 oz fondant icing sugar
pale violet food colouring

1. Preheat the oven to 180°C/350°F/Gas Mark 4 and line a 12-hole muffin tray with deep paper cases.

2. Place the butter, sugar and eggs in a bowl. Sift in the flour and baking powder. Finely grate in the zest from the lemon.

3. Beat together for about 2 minutes with an electric hand mixer until pale and fluffy. Spoon into the paper cases and bake for 20–25 minutes until firm and golden. Cool on a wire rack.

4. To decorate the cupcakes, spread the violets on some nonstick baking parchment. Beat the egg white until frothy, then brush thinly over the violets. Dust with caster sugar and leave to dry out for 2 hours.

5. Beat the icing sugar with the colouring and enough water to give a thin coating consistency. Drizzle over the top of each cupcake quickly and top with a violet. Leave to set for 30 minutes. Store in an airtight container in a cool place for up to 2 days.

Daisy Chain Lemon Cupcakes

Makes 12

125 g/4 oz caster sugar	**To decorate:**
125 g/4 oz soft tub margarine	50 g/2 oz ready-to-roll sugarpaste icing
2 medium eggs	yellow piping icing tube
125 g/4 oz self-raising flour	225 g/8 oz fondant icing sugar
½ tsp baking powder	lemon yellow food colouring
1 tsp lemon juice	

1. Preheat the oven to 190°C/375°F/Gas Mark 5. Line a bun tray with 12 paper cases.

2. Place all the cupcake ingredients in a large bowl and beat with an electric mixer for about 2 minutes until smooth. Fill the paper cases halfway up with the mixture.

3. Bake for about 15 minutes until firm, risen and golden. Remove to a wire rack to cool.

4. Roll out the icing thinly and stamp out small daisies with a fluted daisy cutter. Pipe a small yellow dot of icing into the centre of each and leave to dry out for 1 hour.

5. Blend the fondant icing sugar with a little water and a few dots of yellow colouring to make a thick, easy-to-spread icing, then smooth over the top of each cupcake. Decorate with the cut-out daisies immediately and leave to set for 1 hour. Keep for up to 3 days in an airtight container.

Florentine-topped Cupcakes

Makes 18

150 g/5 oz butter, softened
150 g/5 oz caster sugar
175 g/6 oz self-raising flour
3 medium eggs
1 tsp vanilla extract
75 g/3 oz glacé cherries, chopped
50 g/2 oz angelica, chopped
50 g/2 oz candied peel, chopped
50 g/2 oz dried cranberries

To decorate:
75 g/3 oz plain or milk
   chocolate, melted
50 g/2 oz flaked almonds

1. Preheat the oven to 180°C/350°F/Gas Mark 4. Line two
   12-hole muffin trays with 18 paper cases.

2. Place the butter and sugar in a bowl, then sift in the flour.
   In another bowl, beat the eggs with the vanilla extract, then
   add to the first mixture and beat until smooth.

3. Fold in half the cherries, angelica, peel and cranberries.
   Spoon into the cases, filling them three-quarters full.

4. Bake for about 18 minutes until firm to the touch in the
   centre. Turn out to cool on a wire rack.

5. Spoon a little melted chocolate on top of each cupcake,
   then scatter the remaining cherries, angelica, peel and
   cranberries and the almonds into the wet chocolate. Drizzle
   the remaining chocolate over the fruit topping with a
   teaspoon and leave to set for 30 minutes. Keep for up to
   2 days in an airtight container.

Fondant Fancies

Makes 16–18

150 g/5 oz self-raising flour
150 g/5 oz caster sugar
50 g/2 oz ground almonds
150 g/5 oz butter, softened
3 medium eggs, beaten
4 tbsp milk

To decorate:
450 g/1 lb fondant
  icing sugar
paste food colourings
selection fancy cake
  decorations

1. Preheat the oven to 180°C/350°F/Gas Mark 4. Line two 12-hole bun trays with 16–18 paper cases, depending on the depth of the tray holes.

2. Sift the flour into a bowl and stir in the caster sugar and almonds. Add the butter, eggs and milk and beat until smooth.

3. Spoon into the paper cases and bake for 15–20 minutes until golden and firm to the touch. Turn out to cool on a wire rack. When cool, trim the tops flat if they have peaked slightly.

4. To decorate the cupcakes, make the fondant icing to a thick coating consistency, following the packet instructions. Divide into batches and colour each separately with a little paste food colouring. Keep each bowl covered with a damp cloth until needed. Spoon some icing over each cupcake, being sure to flood it right to the edge. Top each with a fancy decoration and leave to set for 30 minutes. Keep for up to 2 days in a cool place.

Lemon & Cardamom Cupcakes with Mascarpone Topping

Makes 12

1 tsp cardamom seeds
200 g/7 oz butter
50 g/2 oz plain flour
200 g/7 oz self-raising flour
1 tsp baking powder
200 g/7 oz caster sugar
zest of 1 lemon, finely grated
3 medium eggs
100 ml/3½ fl oz natural yogurt
4 tbsp lemon curd

To decorate:
250 g/9 oz tub mascarpone
6 tbsp icing sugar
1 tsp lemon juice
lemon zest strips

1. Preheat the oven to 180°C/350°F/Gas Mark 4. Line a 12-hole muffin tray with deep paper cases. Crush the cardamom seeds and remove the outer cases. Melt the butter and leave aside to cool.

2. Sift the flours and baking powder into a bowl and stir in the crushed seeds, the sugar and the lemon zest.

3. In another bowl, whisk together the eggs and yogurt. Pour into the dry ingredients with the cooled melted butter and beat until combined.

4. Divide half the mixture between the paper cases, put a teaspoon of lemon curd into each, then top with the remaining mixture. Bake for about 25 minutes until golden.

5. To make the topping, beat the mascarpone with the icing sugar and lemon juice. Swirl onto each cupcake and top with lemon strips. Eat fresh on the day of baking once decorated, or store undecorated in an airtight container for up to 2 days and add the topping just before serving.

Chocolate
Indulgence

Chocolate Mud Cupcakes

Makes 16

150 g/5 oz butter, softened
150 g/5 oz golden caster sugar
3 medium eggs, beaten
125 g/4 oz self-raising flour
25 g/1 oz cocoa powder

To decorate:
75 g/3 oz milk chocolate
75 g/3 oz unsalted butter,
  softened
150 g/5 oz golden icing
  sugar, sifted
white and dark chocolate
  sprinkles

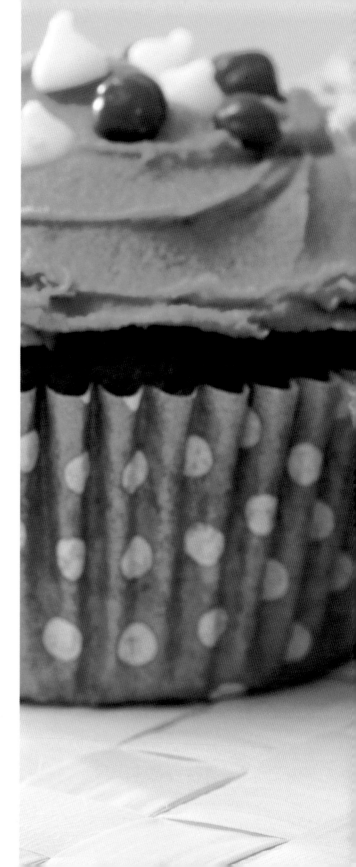

1. Preheat the oven to 190°C/375°F/Gas Mark 5. Line one or two bun trays with 16 foil or paper cases.

2. Place the butter, caster sugar and eggs in a large bowl and then sift in the flour and cocoa powder. Whisk together for about 2 minutes until smooth, then spoon into the cases, filling them two-thirds full.

3. Bake for about 14 minutes until well risen and springy to the touch. Cool on a wire rack.

4. To make the frosting, break the chocolate into squares and melt in a heatproof bowl over a pan of barely simmering water. Set aside to cool. Beat the butter and icing sugar together until fluffy, then whisk in the cooled melted chocolate. Swirl over the cupcakes with a flat-bladed knife. Scatter over the sprinkles. Keep for up to 3 days in a cool place.

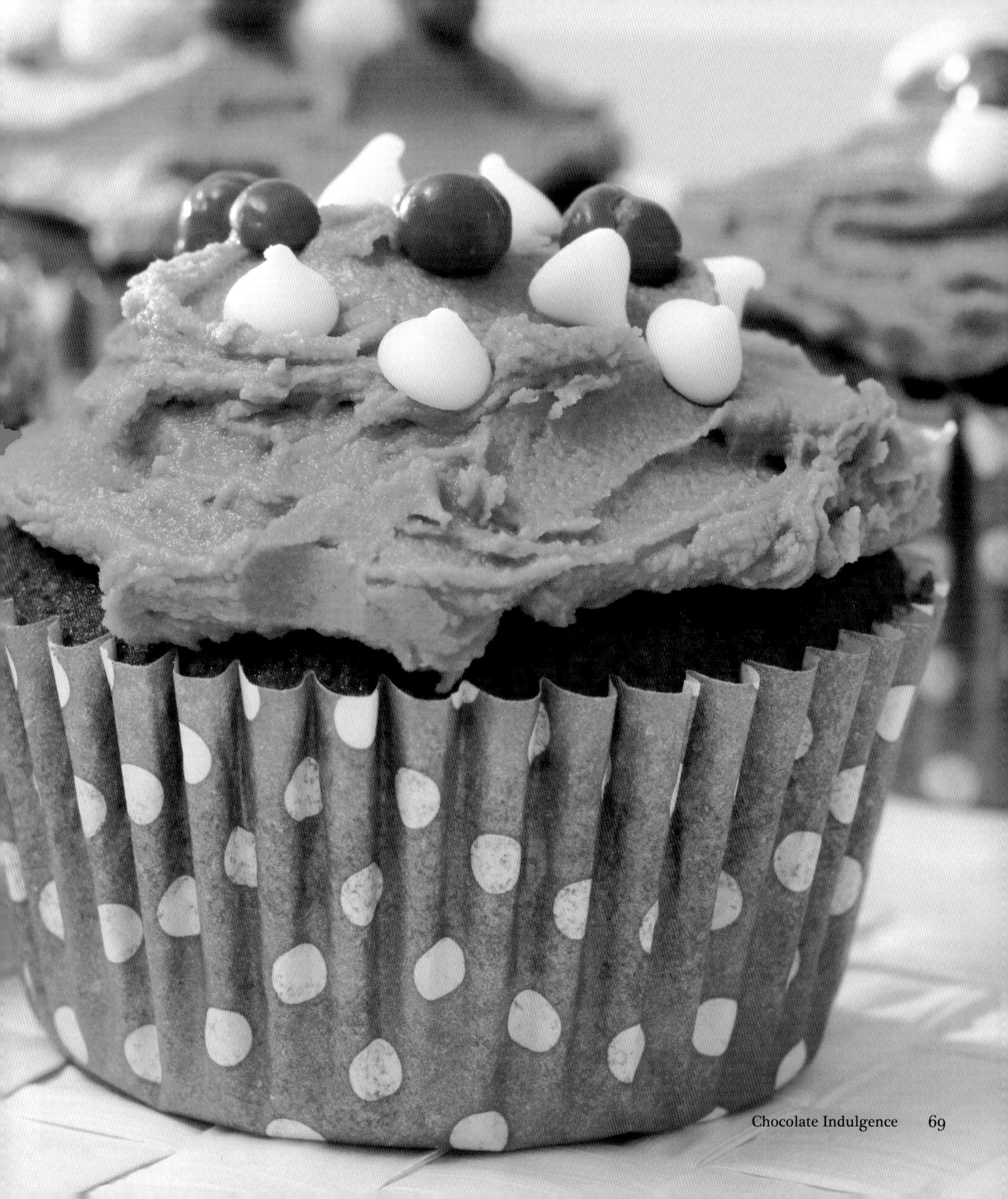

White Chocolate Cupcakes

Makes 12

200 g/7 oz butter
125 g/4 oz white chocolate
50 g/2 oz plain flour
200 g/7 oz self-raising flour
1 tsp baking powder
200 g/7 oz caster sugar
finely grated zest of ½ lemon
3 medium eggs
100 ml/3½ fl oz natural yogurt
250 g/9 oz white chocolate, chopped, to decorate

1. Preheat the oven to 180°C/350°F/Gas Mark 4. Line a 12-hole deep muffin tray with paper cases. Melt the butter and leave aside to cool.

2. Coarsely grate or chop the white chocolate. Sift the flours and baking powder into a bowl and stir in the sugar, lemon zest and chopped white chocolate.

3. In another bowl, whisk together the eggs and yogurt. Pour into the dry ingredients with the cooled melted butter and beat until combined. Spoon into the paper cases and bake for about 25 minutes until firm and golden.

4. To decorate the cupcakes, melt one quarter of the white chocolate in a heatproof bowl standing over a pan of barely simmering water. Spread the melted chocolate out onto a clean plastic board. When almost set, make into curls by pulling a sharp knife through the chocolate (*see* page 35). Refrigerate for 30 minutes to set.

5. Melt the remaining white chocolate, then spoon over the cupcakes and leave for about 10 minutes until cooled and half set. Top each cupcake while still wet with the white chocolate curls and leave to set for 30 minutes. Keep for up to 2 days in the refrigerator.

Double Chocolate Chip Cupcakes

Makes 14

125 g/4 oz soft tub margarine
125 g/4 oz golden caster sugar
2 medium eggs, beaten
25 g/1 oz cocoa powder
175 g/6 oz self-raising flour
1 tsp baking powder
50 g/2 oz milk chocolate chips
50 g/2 oz dark or white chocolate chips
1 tbsp milk

1. Preheat the oven to 180°C/350°F/Gas Mark 4. Line one or two bun trays with 14 small paper cases.

2. Place the margarine and sugar in a large bowl with the eggs and sift in the cocoa powder, flour and baking powder. Beat for about 2 minutes until smooth, then fold in the chocolate chips with the milk.

3. Spoon into the paper cases and bake for 15–20 minutes until firm. Place on a wire rack to cool. Keep for 4–5 days in an airtight container.

Chocolate Fudge Flake Cupcakes

Makes 12

125 g/4 oz self-raising flour
25 g/1 oz cocoa powder
125 g/4 oz soft tub margarine
125 g/4 oz soft light brown sugar
2 medium eggs, beaten
2 tbsp milk

To decorate:
25 g/1 oz butter
50 g/2 oz golden syrup
15 g/½ oz cocoa powder
125 g/4 oz golden icing sugar
25 g/1 oz cream cheese
40 g/1½ oz chocolate flake bars

1. Preheat the oven to 180°C/350°F/Gas Mark 4. Line a 12-hole muffin tray with deep paper cases.

2. Sift the flour and cocoa powder into a large bowl, add the margarine, sugar, eggs and milk and whisk with an electric beater for about 2 minutes until smooth.

3. Divide the mixture between the paper cases and bake for about 20 minutes until a skewer inserted into the middle comes out clean. Turn out to cool on a wire rack.

4. To make the topping, melt the butter with the syrup and cocoa powder in a pan. Cool, then whisk in the icing sugar until the mixture has thickened and beat in the cream cheese. Spread the frosting over the cupcakes. Chop the flake bars into small chunks, then place one chunk in the centre of each cupcake. Keep for 2–3 days in the refrigerator.

Black Forest Cupcakes

Makes 12

1 tbsp cocoa powder
2 tbsp boiling water
175 g/6 oz self-raising flour
1 tsp baking powder
125 g/4 oz soft tub margarine
175 g/6 oz soft dark
  brown sugar
2 medium eggs
3 tbsp milk

To decorate:

125 g/4 oz dark chocolate
4 tbsp seedless raspberry
  jam, warmed
150 ml/¼ pint double
  cream
1 tbsp kirsch (optional)
12 natural-coloured
  glacé cherries

1. Preheat the oven to 180°C/350°F/Gas Mark 4. Line a
   12-hole muffin tray with deep paper cases. Blend the
   cocoa powder with the boiling water and leave to cool.

2. Sift the flour and baking powder into a bowl and add the
   margarine, sugar, eggs, milk and the cocoa mixture. Whisk
   together for about 2 minutes until smooth, then spoon
   into the paper cases.

3. Bake for 15–20 minutes until springy to the touch.
   Cool in the trays for 5 minutes, then turn out onto a wire
   rack to cool.

4. To decorate the cupcakes, melt the chocolate and spread
   it out to cool on a clean plastic board. When it is almost
   set, pull a sharp knife through the chocolate to make
   curls. Refrigerate these until needed. Brush the top of
   each cupcake with a little raspberry jam. Whisk the cream
   until it forms soft peaks, then fold in the kirsch, if using.
   Pipe or swirl the cream on top of each cupcake. Top with
   chocolate curls and whole glacé cherries for the large
   muffins or halved cherries for the smaller ones. Eat fresh,
   or keep for 1 day in the refrigerator.

Mocha Cupcakes

Makes 12

125 g/4 oz soft tub margarine
125 g/4 oz golden caster sugar
150 g/5 oz self-raising flour
2 tbsp cocoa powder
2 medium eggs
1 tbsp golden syrup
2 tbsp milk

To decorate:
225 g/8 oz golden icing sugar
125 g/4 oz unsalted butter, softened
2 tsp coffee extract
12 Cape gooseberries, papery
  covering pulled back

1. Preheat the oven to 180°C/350°F/Gas Mark 4. Line a
   12-hole muffin tray with deep paper cases.

2. Place the margarine and sugar in a large bowl, then sift
   in the flour and cocoa powder.

3. In another bowl, beat the eggs with the syrup, then
   add to the cocoa mixture. Whisk everything together
   with the milk using an electric beater for 2 minutes,
   or by hand with a wooden spoon.

4. Divide the mixture between the cases, filling them
   three-quarters full. Bake for about 20 minutes until the
   centres are springy to the touch. Turn out to cool on
   a wire rack.

5. Make the frosting by sifting the icing sugar into a bowl.
   Add the butter, coffee extract and 1 tbsp hot water. Beat
   until fluffy, then swirl onto each cupcake with a flat-bladed
   knife. Top each with a fresh Cape gooseberry. Keep
   for up to 2 days in a cool place.

Chocolate & Cranberry Cupcakes

Makes 12

125 g/4 oz soft tub margarine
125 g/4 oz golden caster
  sugar
2 medium eggs
175 g/6 oz self-raising flour
25 g/1 oz cocoa powder
1 tsp baking powder
2 tbsp milk
125 g/4 oz milk chocolate chips
50 g/2 oz dried cranberries

To decorate:
25 g/1 oz cocoa powder
40 g/1½ oz unsalted butter
125 g/4 oz golden icing
  sugar
25 g/1 oz dried cranberries

1. Preheat the oven to 180°C/350°F/Gas Mark 4. Line a muffin tray with 12 deep paper cases.

2. Place the margarine, sugar and eggs in a bowl, then sift in the flour, cocoa powder and baking powder. Add the milk and beat until smooth, then fold in the chocolate chips and cranberries.

3. Spoon into the paper cases and bake for 15–20 minutes until firm in the centre. Remove to a wire rack to cool.

4. To decorate the cupcakes, blend the cocoa powder with 1 tbsp hot water until smooth. Cool for 5 minutes. Beat the butter and icing sugar together and then beat in the cocoa mixture.

5. Place in a piping bag with a plain nozzle and pipe swirls on top of each cupcake. Top with dried cranberries. Keep for 2–3 days in the refrigerator.

Rocky Road Cupcakes

Makes 14–18

125 g/4 oz self-raising flour
25 g/1 oz cocoa powder
125 g/4 oz soft dark brown sugar
125 g/4 oz soft tub margarine
2 medium eggs, beaten
2 tbsp milk

To decorate:
75 g/3 oz dark chocolate,
    broken into squares
40 g/1½ oz butter
75 g/3 oz mini marshmallows
40 g/1½ oz chopped mixed nuts

1. Preheat the oven to 180°C/350°F/Gas Mark 4. Line bun trays with 14–18 paper cases or silicone cupcake moulds, depending on the depth of the holes.

2. Sift the flour and cocoa powder into a large bowl. Add the sugar, margarine, eggs and milk and whisk with an electric beater for about 2 minutes until smooth.

3. Divide the mixture evenly between the paper cases and bake for about 20 minutes until a skewer inserted into the middle comes out clean. Remove the tray from the oven, but leave the oven on.

4. To make the topping, gently melt the chocolate and butter together in a small pan over a low heat. Place the melted chocolate mixture in an icing bag made of greaseproof paper and snip away the end. Pipe a little of the mixture on top of each cupcake, then scatter the marshmallows and nuts over each one and return to the oven. Bake for 2–3 minutes to soften the marshmallows. Remove from the oven and pipe the remaining chocolate over the marshmallows. Leave to cool in the trays for 5 minutes, then remove to cool on a wire rack. Serve warm or cold. Keep for up to 2 days in an airtight container.

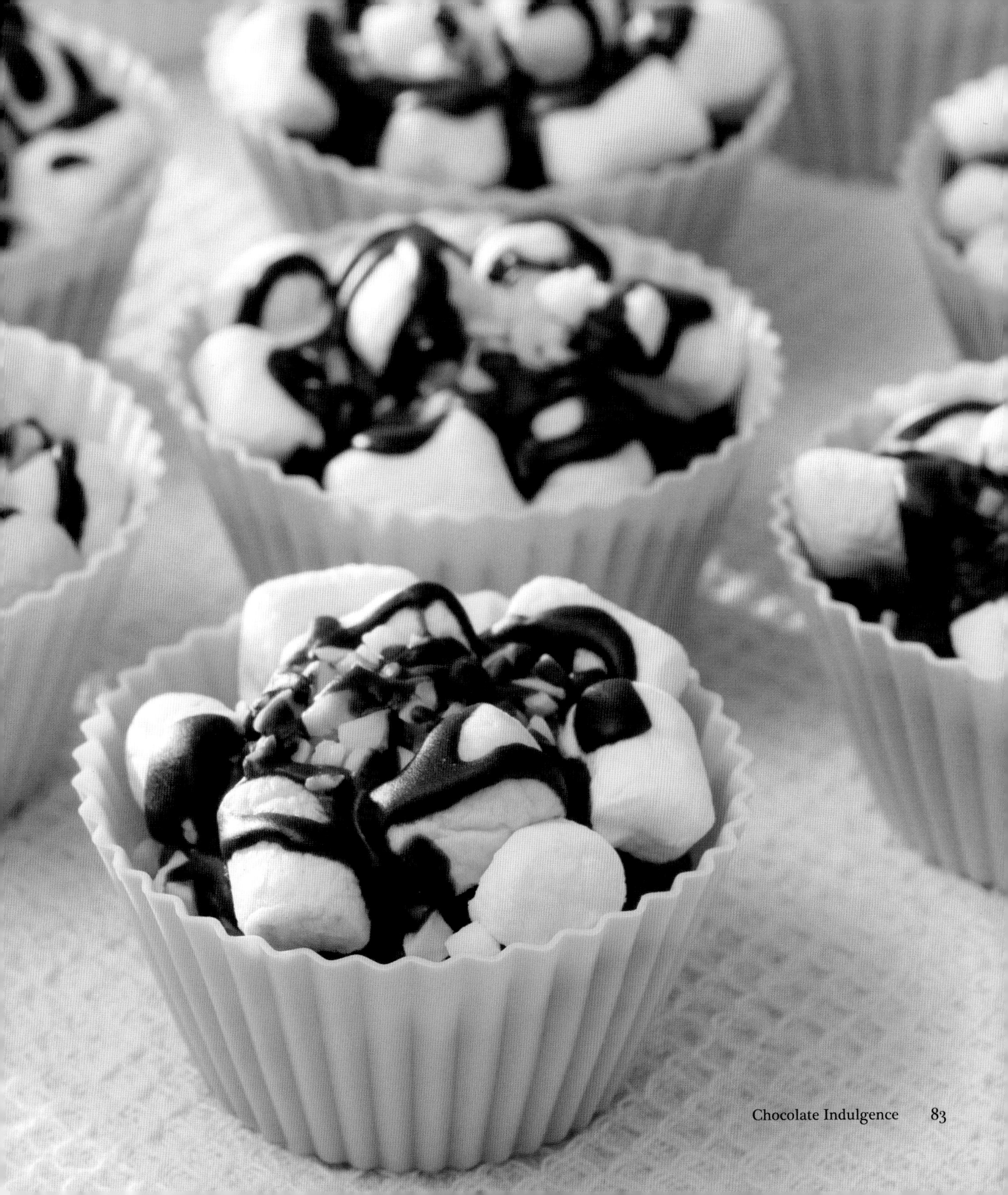

Chocolate & Orange Marbled Muffins

Makes 10–12

175 g/6 oz soft tub margarine
175 g/6 oz caster sugar
3 medium eggs
175 g/6 oz self-raising flour
1 tsp baking powder
1 tbsp cocoa powder
finely grated zest and juice of ½ orange
4 tbsp clear honey, to glaze

1. Preheat the oven to 180°C/350°F/Gas Mark 4. Grease two deep 6-hole muffin trays, or line with 10–12 deep paper cases, depending on the depth of the holes.

2. Put the margarine, sugar, eggs, flour and baking powder into a large mixing bowl. Whisk the mixture together for about 2 minutes until smooth.

3. Place half the mixture into another bowl and sift over the cocoa powder, then stir in until blended. Stir the orange juice and zest into the other mixture.

4. Spoon the cocoa mixture evenly between the prepared trays. Spoon over the orange mixture and, using a flat-bladed knife, swirl through the two mixtures to make a marbled pattern.

5. Bake for 15–20 minutes until well risen and firm to the touch. Cool in the trays for 5 minutes, then turn out to cool on a wire rack. While still warm, drizzle each muffin with a little clear honey. Keep for up to 4 days in an airtight container.

Mint Choc Chip Cupcakes

Makes 12

125 g/4 oz soft tub margarine
125 g/4 oz golden caster sugar
2 medium eggs
175 g/6 oz self-raising flour
25 g/1 oz cocoa powder
1 tsp baking powder
75 g/3 oz dark chocolate chips
25 g/1 oz clear hard peppermint
  sweets, crushed into crumbs

To decorate:
50 g/2 oz unsalted butter
175 g/6 oz icing sugar
peppermint flavouring or extract
green food colouring
50 g/2 oz chocolate squares

1. Preheat the oven to 180°C/350°F/Gas Mark 4. Line a 12-hole
   muffin tray with deep paper cases.

2. Place the margarine, sugar and eggs in a bowl, then sift in the
   flour, cocoa powder and baking powder. Beat by hand or with
   an electric mixer until smooth, then fold in the chocolate chips
   and the crushed mints.

3. Spoon the mixture into the paper cases and bake for 15–20
   minutes until firm in the centre. Remove to a wire rack to cool.

4. Beat the butter and icing sugar together with 1 tbsp warm water,
   the peppermint extract and the food colouring. Place in a piping
   bag with a star nozzle and pipe swirls on top of each cupcake.
   Cut the chocolate into triangles and place one on top of each
   cake. Keep for 3–4 days in an airtight container in a cool place.

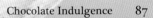

Chocolate & Toffee Cupcakes

Makes 12–14

125 g/4 oz soft fudge
125 g/4 oz soft tub margarine
125 g/4 oz golden caster sugar
150 g/5 oz self-raising flour
2 tbsp cocoa powder
2 medium eggs
1 tbsp golden syrup
1 batch cream cheese frosting
  (*see* page 29), to decorate

1. Preheat the oven to 180°C/350°F/Gas Mark 4. Line one or two bun trays with 12–14 paper cases, depending on the depth of the holes. Cut one quarter of the fudge into slices for decoration. Chop the rest into small cubes. Set all the fudge aside.

2. Place the margarine and the sugar in a large bowl and then sift in the flour and cocoa powder. In another bowl, beat the eggs with the syrup, then add to the flour mixture. Whisk together with an electric beater for 2 minutes, or by hand with a wooden spoon until smooth. Gently fold in the fudge cubes.

3. Spoon the mixture into the cases, filling them three-quarters full. Bake for about 15 minutes until a skewer inserted into the centre comes out clean. Turn out to cool on a wire rack.

4. Swirl the cream cheese frosting over each cupcake, then finish by topping with a fudge slice. Keep for 3–4 days chilled in a sealed container.

Cappuccino Cupcakes

Makes 12–14

125 g/4 oz soft tub margarine
125 g/4 oz golden caster sugar
150 g/5 oz self-raising flour
2 tbsp cocoa powder
2 medium eggs
1 tbsp golden syrup
50 g/2 oz finely grated chocolate

To decorate:
150 ml/¼ pint double cream
½ tsp coffee extract
chocolate sprinkles

1. Preheat the oven to 180°C/350°F/Gas Mark 4. Line one or two bun trays with 12–14 paper cases or silicone moulds, depending on the depth of the holes.

2. Place the margarine and the sugar in a large bowl, then sift in the flour and cocoa powder.

3. In another bowl, beat the eggs with the syrup, then add to the flour mixture. Whisk together with an electric beater for 2 minutes, or by hand with a wooden spoon, until smooth and then fold in the grated chocolate.

4. Divide the mixture between the cases, filling them three-quarters full. Bake for about 20 minutes until springy to the touch in the centre. Turn out to cool on a wire rack.

5. To decorate, whisk the cream until it forms soft peaks and whisk in the coffee extract, then swirl over the tops of the muffins with a small palette knife. Scatter the tops with chocolate sprinkles to serve. Eat on the day of decorating, or keep for 1 day in a sealed container in the refrigerator.

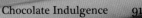

Chunky Chocolate Cupcakes

Makes 12–14

	To decorate:
125 g/4 oz soft tub margarine	75 g/3 oz granulated
125 g/4 oz golden caster sugar	sugar
2 medium eggs, beaten	5 tbsp evaporated milk
25 g/1 oz cocoa powder	125 g/4 oz dark
175 g/6 oz self-raising flour	chocolate, chopped
1 tsp baking powder	40 g/1½ oz unsalted
2 tbsp milk	butter
50 g/2 oz milk chocolate,	
chopped	
50 g/2 oz dark or white	
chocolate, chopped	

1. Make the frosting first in order to allow it to cool. Place the sugar and evaporated milk in a heavy-based pan and stir over a low heat until every grain of sugar has dissolved. Simmer for 5 minutes but do not allow the mixture to boil. Remove from the heat, cool for 5 minutes and then add the chocolate and butter. Stir until these melt. Pour the mixture into a bowl and chill for 2 hours until thickened.

2. Preheat the oven to 180°C/350°F/Gas Mark 4. Line one or two deep muffin trays with 12–14 paper cases, depending on the depth of the holes. Place the margarine and sugar in a bowl with the eggs and sift in the cocoa powder, flour and baking powder. Beat with the milk for about 2 minutes until smooth, then fold in the chopped chocolate. Spoon into the paper cases and bake for 15–20 minutes until firm. Place on a wire rack to cool.

3. Remove the frosting from the fridge and beat to soften it slightly. Swirl it over the muffins. Keep in a cool place in a sealed container for 3–4 days.

Very Rich Chocolate Cupcakes

Makes 12–14

75 g/3 oz self-raising flour
25 g/1 oz cocoa powder
75 g/3 oz soft dark brown sugar
75 g/3 oz butter, softened
3 medium eggs
2 tbsp milk

To decorate:
200 g/7 oz dark
  chocolate
100 ml/3½ fl oz
  whipping cream
1 tbsp liquid glucose
selection chocolate
  decorations

1. Preheat the oven to 190°C/350°F/Gas Mark 5. Line one or two 12-hole bun trays with 12–14 paper cases, depending on the depth of the holes.

2. Sift the flour and cocoa powder into a bowl and add the sugar, butter, eggs and milk. Whisk until smooth, then spoon into the paper cases.

3. Bake for about 14 minutes until just firm to the touch in the centre. Transfer to a wire rack to cool.

4. To decorate the cupcakes, break the chocolate into pieces and melt in a heatproof bowl standing over a pan of warm water.

5. In another pan, bring the cream to just below boiling, then remove from the heat and stir in the liquid glucose. Add the melted chocolate and stir until smooth and glossy. Spoon over the cupcakes and immediately top each with a chocolate decoration. Leave to set for 30 minutes. Keep for up to 3 days in an airtight container in a cool place.

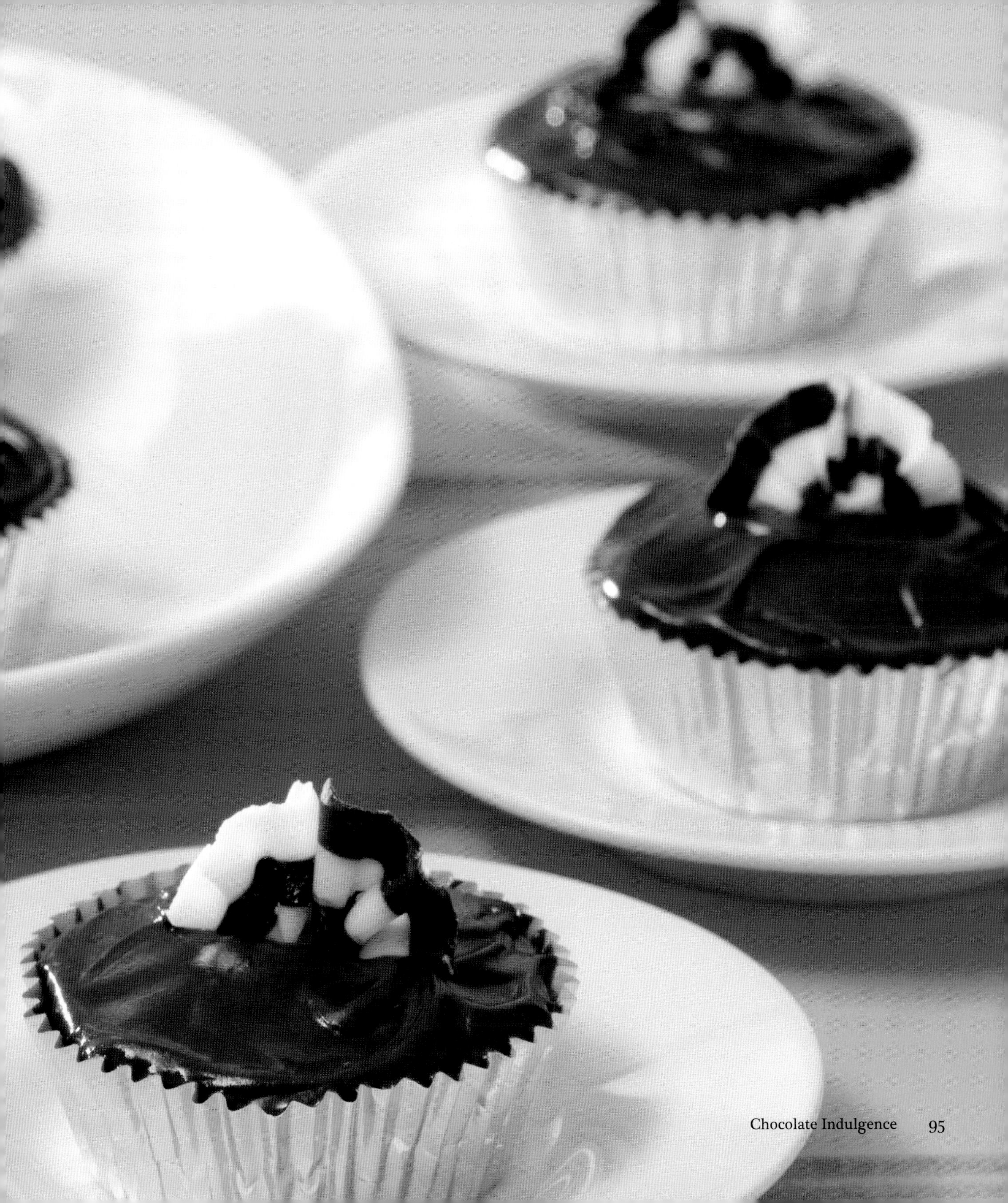

Orange Drizzle Cupcakes

Makes 10

75 g/3 oz dark chocolate, chopped
125 g/4 oz butter
125 g/4 oz caster sugar
2 medium eggs, beaten
200 g/7 oz self-raising flour
zest of ½ orange, finely grated
5 tbsp thick natural yogurt

To decorate:
finely grated zest and
 1 tbsp juice from
 1 small orange
1 batch buttercream
 (*see* page 29)
2 tbsp marmalade

1. Preheat the oven to 190°C/375°F/Gas Mark 5. Grease 10 deep muffin moulds or line a 12-hole muffin tray with 10 deep paper cases.

2. Melt the chocolate in a heatproof bowl over a pan of warm water or in the microwave oven on low in bursts of 30 seconds and leave to cool.

3. Put the butter and sugar in a large bowl and whisk until light and fluffy. Gradually beat in the eggs, adding a teaspoon of flour with each addition. Beat in the cooled melted chocolate, then sift in the flour. Add the orange zest and yogurt to the bowl and whisk until smooth.

4. Spoon the mixture into the paper cases and bake for about 25 minutes until well risen and springy to the touch. Leave for 2 minutes in the moulds or tray, then turn out onto a wire rack.

5. To decorate, mix the orange zest and juice into the buttercream and use to fill a piping bag fitted with a star nozzle. Pipe swirls of buttercream on top of each cupcake. Warm the marmalade and place small drizzles over the cupcakes with a teaspoon. Keep in an airtight container in a cool place for up to 4 days.

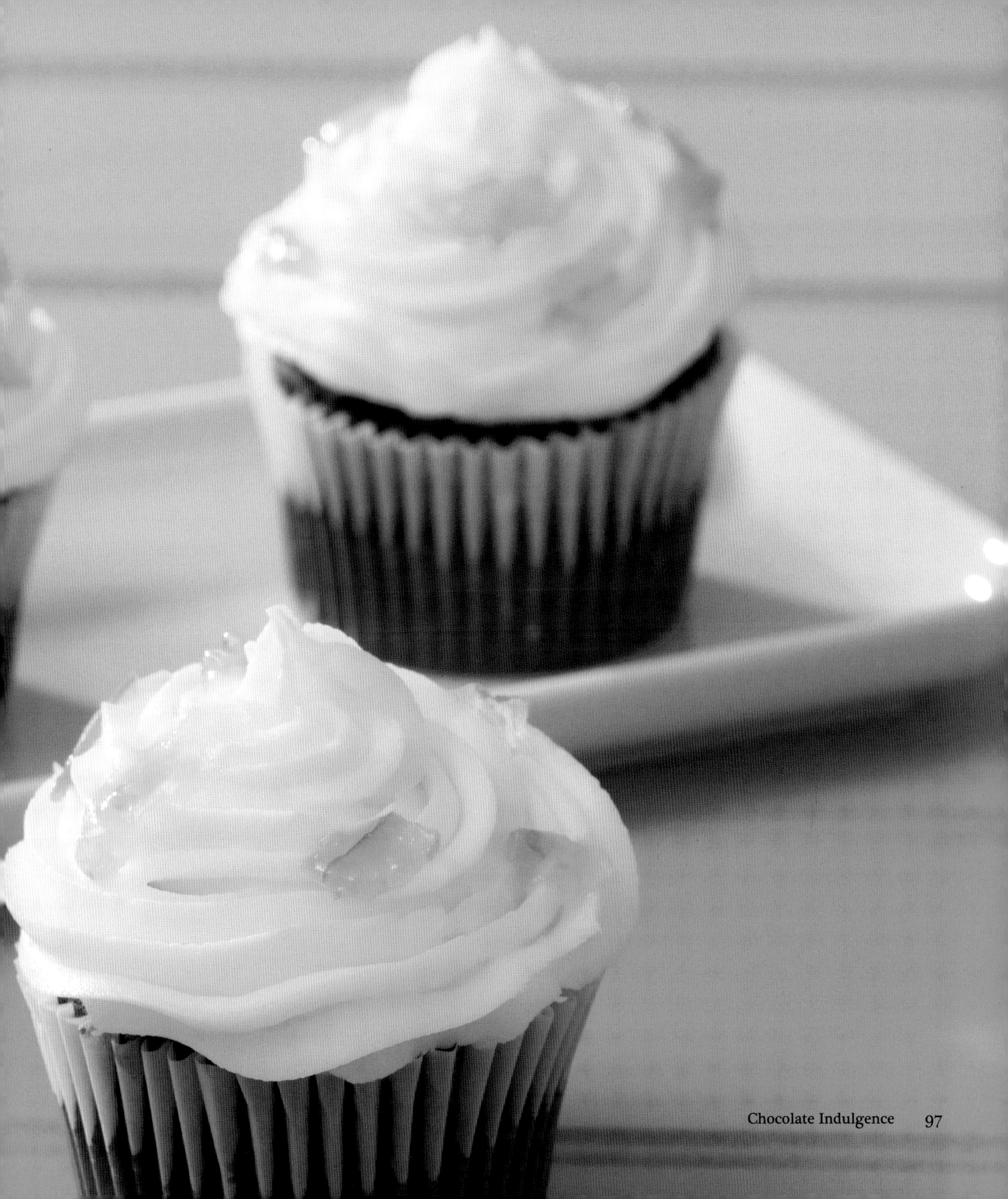

Parties &
Celebration

Boys' & Girls' Names

Makes 16–18

175 g/6 oz self-raising flour
175 g/6 oz caster sugar
175 g/6 oz soft tub margarine
3 medium eggs, beaten
1 tsp vanilla extract

To decorate:
1 batch buttercream
  (*see* page 29)
paste food colourings
sprinkles and decorations
gel writing icing tubes

1. Preheat the oven to 180°C/350°F/Gas Mark 4. Line two 12-hole bun trays with 16–18 paper fairy-cake cases or silicone moulds, depending on the depth of the holes.

2. Sift the flour into a bowl and stir together with the caster sugar. Add the margarine, eggs and vanilla extract and beat together for about 2 minutes until smooth.

3. Spoon into the cases and bake for 15–20 minutes until golden and firm to the touch. Turn out on a wire rack. When cool, trim the tops flat if they have peaked slightly.

4. Divide the buttercream into batches and colour pink, green and yellow. Spread the icing over the cakes. Coat the edges of each fairy cake with brightly coloured sprinkles or decorations, then add a name in the centre of each one with the writing icing. Keep in an airtight container in a cool place for up to 2 days.

Pirate Cupcakes

Makes 14–16

125 g/4 oz self-raising
 flour
125 g/4 oz caster sugar
125 g/4 oz soft
 margarine
2 medium eggs, beaten
1 tsp vanilla extract

To decorate:
125 g/4 oz buttercream
 (*see* page 29)
450 g/1 lb ready-to-roll sugarpaste
pink, yellow, blue and black paste
 food colourings
icing sugar, for dusting
small sweets and edible
 coloured balls
small tube red gel icing

1. Preheat the oven to 180°C/350°F/Gas Mark 4. Line two 12-hole bun trays with 14–16 paper fairy-cake cases or silicone moulds, depending on the depth of the holes.

2. Sift the flour into a bowl and stir together with the caster sugar. Add the margarine, eggs and vanilla extract and beat together for about 2 minutes until smooth. Divide the mixture between the cases and bake for 15–20 minutes until golden and firm to the touch. Turn out on a wire rack. When cool, trim the tops flat if they have peaked slightly.

3. To decorate, lightly coat the top of each cupcake with a little buttercream. Colour the sugarpaste pale pink and roll out thinly on a surface dusted with icing sugar. Stamp or cut out circles 6 cm/2½ inches wide and place these on the buttercream to cover the top of each cupcake.

4. Colour some scraps of sugarpaste blue, some yellow and a small amount black. Make triangular shapes from the blue and yellow icing and place these onto the pink icing at an angle to form hats. Stick edible coloured balls into the icing to decorate the hats. Make thin sausages from black sugarpaste and press these across the cupcakes, then make tiny black eye patches. Stick on a tiny sweet for each eye and pipe on red mouths with the gel icing. Keep for up to 2 days in an airtight container.

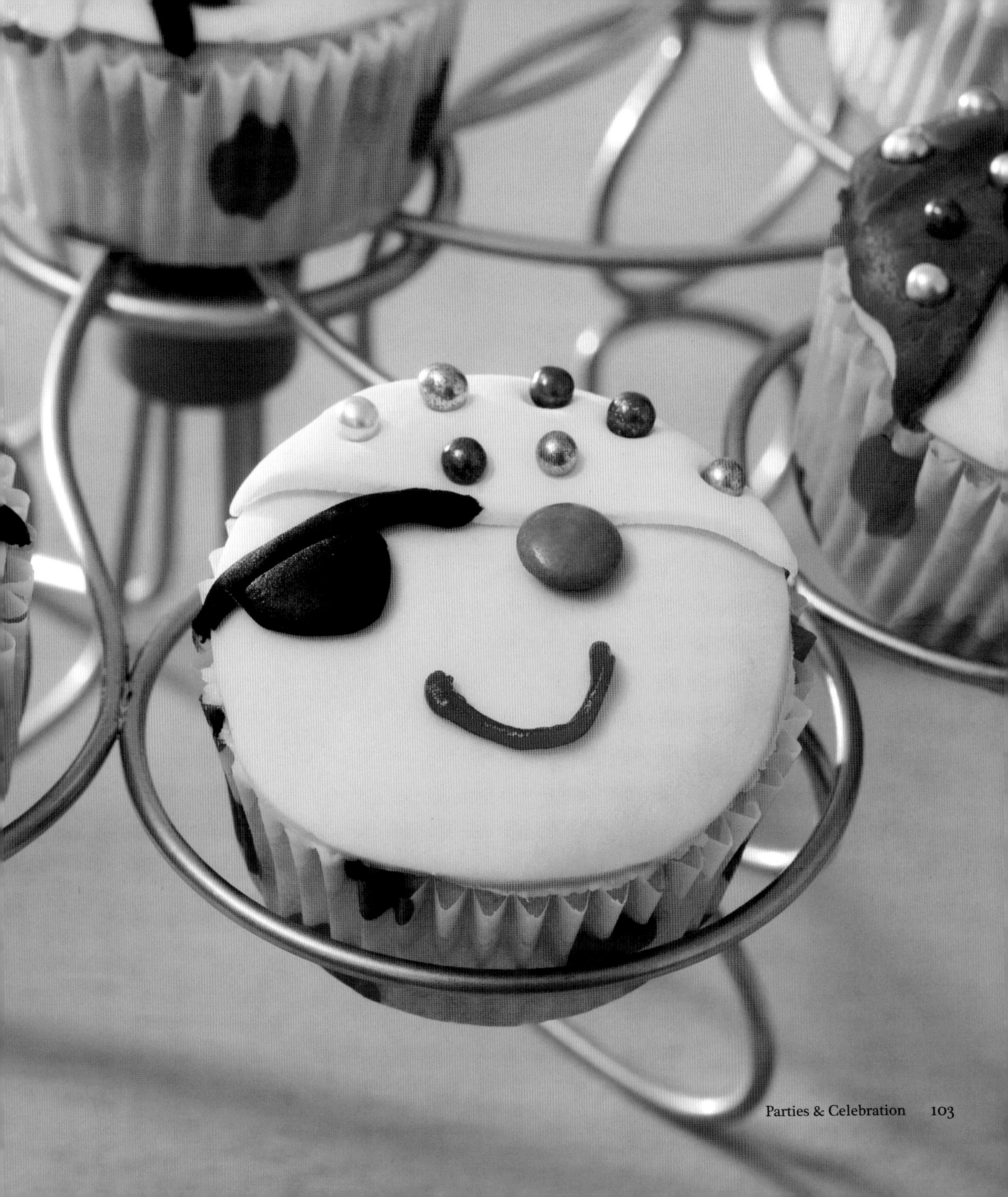

Birthday Numbers Cupcakes

Makes 12–14

125 g/4 oz self-raising flour
125 g/4 oz caster sugar
125 g/4 oz soft tub margarine
2 medium eggs, beaten
1 tsp vanilla extract

To decorate:
225 g/8 oz ready-to-roll sugarpaste
paste food colourings
icing sugar, for dusting
1 batch buttercream (*see* page 29)
small candles

1. Preheat the oven to 180°C/350°F/Gas Mark 4. Line one or
   two 12-hole bun trays with 12–14 paper fairy-cake cases or
   silicone moulds, depending on the depth of the holes.

2. Sift the flour into a bowl and stir together with the caster sugar.
   Add the margarine, eggs and vanilla extract and beat together
   for about 2 minutes until smooth.

3. Spoon into the cases and bake for 15–20 minutes until golden
   and firm to the touch. Turn out on a wire rack. When cool, trim
   the tops flat if they have peaked slightly.

4. To decorate, colour batches of sugarpaste in bright colours. Dust
   a clean surface lightly with icing sugar. Thinly roll each colour
   of sugarpaste and cut out numbers by hand or using a set of
   cutters. Leave these for 2 hours to dry and harden.

5. Using a palette knife, spread the buttercream thickly onto
   the top of each cupcake. Place a small candle into each
   cupcake and stand the number up against this. Serve within
   8 hours, as the numbers may start to soften.

Starry Cupcakes

Makes 12

125 g/4 oz butter, softened
125 g/4 oz caster sugar
125 g/4 oz self-raising flour
2 medium eggs
1 tsp vanilla extract

To decorate:
icing sugar, for dusting
225 g/8 oz ready-to-roll sugarpaste
dust or paste food colourings
1 batch cream cheese frosting (*see* page 29)
edible silver ball decorations (optional)
small candles

1. Preheat the oven to 180°C/350°F/Gas Mark 4. Line a
   12-hole muffin tray with deep paper cases.

2. Place the butter and sugar in a bowl, then sift in the flour.
   In another bowl, beat the eggs with the vanilla extract,
   then add to the flour mixture. Beat until smooth, then
   spoon into the cases, filling them three-quarters full.

3. Bake for about 18 minutes until firm to the touch in the
   centre. Turn out to cool on a wire rack.

4. To decorate the cupcakes, dust a clean flat surface with
   icing sugar. Colour the sugarpaste in batches of bright
   colours, such as blue, yellow and orange. Roll each out
   thinly and cut out stars. Leave to dry out for 2 hours until
   firm. Place the frosting in a piping bag fitted with a star
   nozzle and pipe large swirls on top of each cupcake.
   Decorate each cupcake with stars, edible silver balls, if
   using, and small candles. Keep for up to 2 days in an
   airtight container in a cool place.

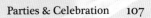

New Home Cupcakes

Makes 14

125 g/4 oz self-raising flour	**To decorate:**
125 g/4 oz caster sugar	125 g/4 oz buttercream (*see* page 29)
125 g/4 oz soft tub margarine	icing sugar, for dusting
2 medium eggs, beaten	450 g/1 lb ready-to-roll sugarpaste
1 tsp vanilla extract	red, brown and yellow paste food colourings
	gel writing icing tubes

1. Preheat the oven to 180°C/350°F/Gas Mark 4. Line two 12-hole bun trays with 14 paper fairy-cake cases or silicone moulds.

2. Sift the flour into a bowl and stir together with the caster sugar. Add the margarine, eggs and vanilla extract and beat together for about 2 minutes until smooth.

3. Spoon into the cases and bake for 15–20 minutes until golden and firm to the touch. Turn out on a wire rack. When cool, trim the tops flat if they have peaked slightly and lightly coat the top of each cupcake with a little buttercream.

4. To decorate, dust a clean flat surface with icing sugar. Colour half the sugarpaste a pale lemon yellow and roll it out thinly. Cut out circles 6 cm/2½ inches wide and place these over the buttercream and press to smooth down. Colour half the remaining icing brown and the other half red. Roll out thinly on a dusted surface. Cut out small squares in the brown icing and triangular roof shapes in red icing. Press the shapes onto the cupcakes and pipe on doors, windows and roof tiles in white writing icing. Keep for up to 3 days in an airtight container.

Polka Dot Cupcakes

Makes 12

150 g/5 oz butter, softened
150 g/5 oz caster sugar
175 g/6 oz self-raising flour
3 medium eggs
1 tsp vanilla extract
2 tbsp milk

To decorate:
1 batch cream cheese
  frosting (*see* page 29)
125 g/4 oz ready-to-roll
  sugarpaste
paste food colourings

1. Preheat the oven to 180°C/350°F/Gas Mark 4. Line a 12-hole muffin tray with paper cases.

2. Place the butter and sugar in a bowl, then sift in the flour. In another bowl, beat the eggs with the vanilla extract and milk, then add to the flour mixture and beat until smooth. Spoon into the cases, filling them three-quarters full.

3. Bake for about 18 minutes until firm to the touch in the centre. Turn out to cool on a wire rack.

4. To decorate the cupcakes, swirl the top of each cupcake with a little cream cheese frosting using a small palette knife. Divide the sugarpaste into batches and colour each one separately with paste food colouring. Dust a clean flat surface with icing sugar. Roll out the coloured icing and stamp out small coloured circles with the flat end of an icing nozzle. Press the dots onto the frosting. Keep for up to 3 days in a cool place in an airtight container.

Valentine Heart Cupcakes

Makes 12

150 g/5 oz butter, softened
150 g/5 oz caster sugar
3 medium eggs, beaten
1 tsp vanilla extract
2 tbsp milk
150 g /5 oz self-raising flour
½ tsp baking powder

To decorate:
pink and red paste food colourings
225 g/8 oz ready-to-roll sugarpaste
icing sugar, for dusting
1 batch cream cheese frosting
 (*see* page 29)

1. Preheat the oven to 180°C/350°F/Gas Mark 4 and line a
   12-hole muffin tray with deep paper cases.

2. Place the butter, sugar, eggs, vanilla extract and milk in a
   bowl, then sift in the flour and baking powder. Beat
   together for about 2 minutes with an electric hand
   mixer until pale and fluffy. Spoon into the paper cases
   and bake for 20–25 minutes until firm and golden. Cool
   on a wire rack.

3. To decorate, colour one third of the sugarpaste pink and
   one third red, leaving the rest white. Dust a clean flat
   surface with icing sugar. Roll out the sugarpaste thinly
   and cut out pink, red and white heart shapes, then leave
   to dry flat and harden for 2 hours.

4. Colour the cream cheese icing pale pink and place in a
   piping bag fitted with a star nozzle. Pipe a swirl on top of
   each cupcake and decorate with the hearts. Keep in a
   cool place for up to 2 days.

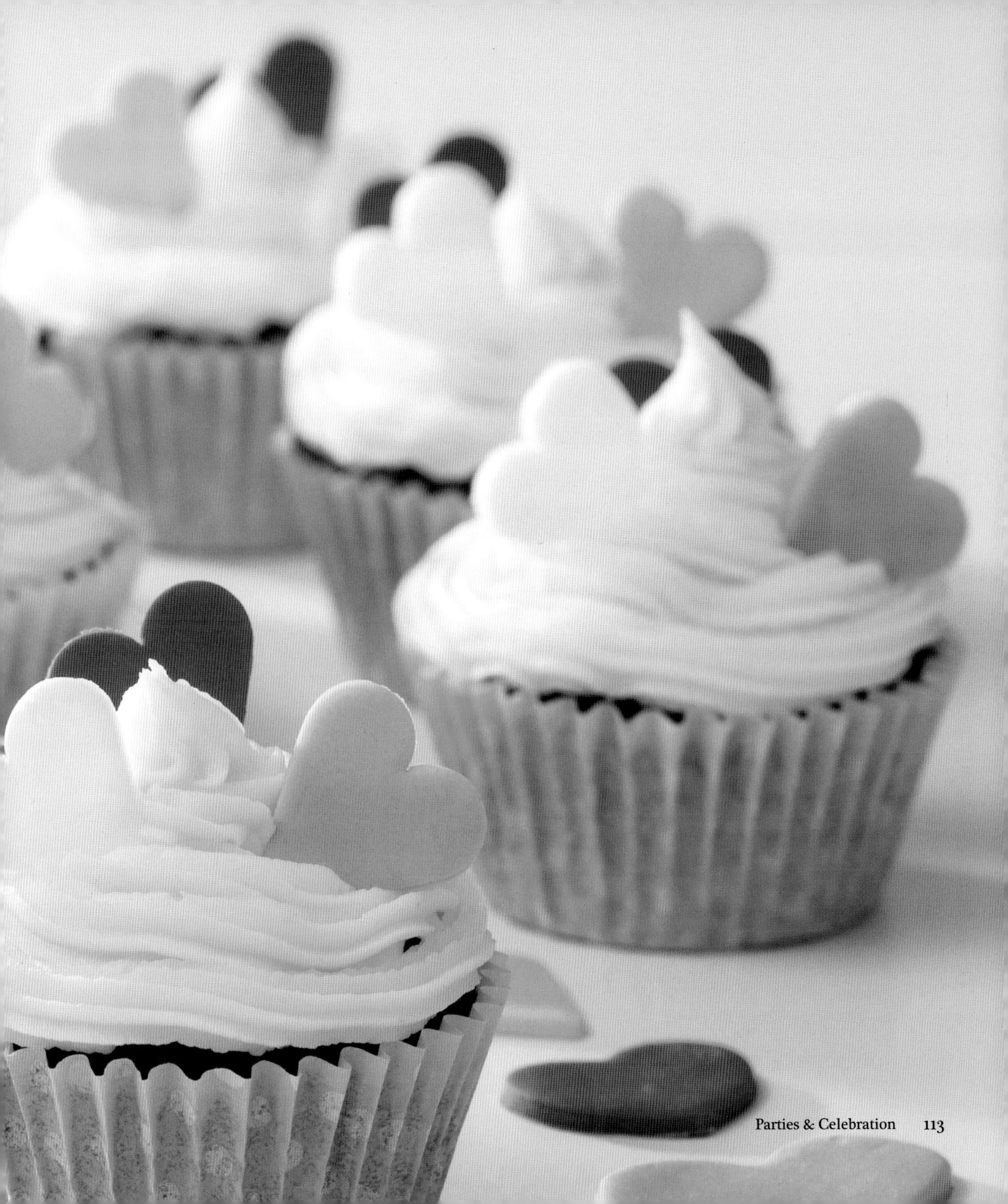

Mother's Day Rose Cupcakes

Makes 12

	To decorate:
125 g/4 oz caster sugar	50 g/2 oz ready-to-roll
125 g/4 oz soft tub margarine	sugarpaste
2 medium eggs	pink paste food colouring
125 g/4 oz self-raising flour	350 g/12 oz fondant
1 tsp baking powder	icing sugar
1 tsp rosewater	

1. Preheat the oven to 190°C/375°F/Gas Mark 5. Line a 12-hole bun tray with paper cases.

2. Place all the cupcake ingredients in a large bowl and beat with an electric mixer for about 2 minutes until smooth. Fill the paper cases halfway up with the mixture. Bake for about 15 minutes until firm, risen and golden. Remove to a wire rack to cool.

3. To decorate the cupcakes, first line an egg box with foil and set aside. Colour the sugarpaste with pink paste food colouring. Make a small cone shape, then roll a pea-sized piece of sugarpaste into a ball. Flatten out the ball into a petal shape and wrap this round the cone shape. Continue adding more petals to make a rose, then trim the thick base, place in the egg box and leave to dry out for 2 hours.

4. Blend the fondant icing sugar with a little water to make a thick icing of spreading consistency, then colour this pale pink. Smooth over the top of each cupcake and decorate with the roses immediately. Leave to set for 1 hour. Keep for 1 day in an airtight container.

Father's Day Cupcakes

Makes 14

125 g/4 oz self-raising
  flour
125 g/4 oz caster sugar
125 g/4 oz soft
  tub margarine
2 medium eggs, beaten
1 tsp vanilla extract

To decorate:
1 batch buttercream (*see* page 29)
blue, yellow and orange paste
  food colourings
icing sugar, for dusting
225 g/8 oz ready-to-roll
  sugarpaste
50 g/2 oz royal icing sugar
edible silver balls

1. Preheat the oven to 180°C/350°F/Gas Mark 4. Line two 12-hole bun trays with 14 paper fairy-cake cases or silicone moulds.

2. Sift the flour into a bowl and stir together with the caster sugar. Add the margarine, eggs and vanilla extract and beat together for about 2 minutes until smooth.

3. Spoon into the cases and bake for 15–20 minutes until golden and firm to the touch. Turn out on a wire rack. When cool, trim the tops flat if they have peaked slightly.

4. To decorate, colour half the buttercream yellow and the other half orange and swirl over the top of each cupcake. Dust a clean flat surface with icing sugar. Colour the sugarpaste light blue and roll out thinly. Stamp out large stars 4 cm/1½ inches wide and place these on the buttercream.

5. Make up the royal icing mix and place in a paper piping bag with the end snipped away and pipe 'Dad' or names on the stars. Decorate with the edible silver balls. Keep for up to 3 days in an airtight container.

Butterfly Wings & Flowers Cupcakes

Makes 12–14

150 g/5 oz butter, softened
150 g/5 oz caster sugar
175 g/6 oz self-raising flour
3 medium eggs, beaten
1 tsp lemon juice
2 tbsp milk

To decorate:
350 g/12 oz ready-to-roll sugarpaste
paste food colourings
icing sugar, for dusting
1 batch cream cheese frosting (see page 29)
gel icing tubes

1. Preheat the oven to 180°C/350°F/Gas Mark 4. Line one or two 12-hole muffin trays with 12–14 deep paper cases, depending on the depth of the holes.

2. Place the butter and sugar in a bowl, then sift in the flour. Add the beaten eggs to the bowl with the lemon juice and milk and beat until smooth. Spoon into the cases, filling them three-quarters full.

3. Bake for about 18 minutes until firm to the touch in the centre. Turn out to cool on a wire rack.

4. To decorate, colour the sugarpaste in batches of lilac, blue, pink and yellow. Dust a clean flat surface with icing sugar. Roll out the sugarpaste thinly and mark out butterfly wings, and daisy shapes with a fluted daisy cutter. Leave these to dry for 30 minutes until firm enough to handle.

5. Place the frosting in a piping bag fitted with a star nozzle and pipe swirls onto each cupcake. Press the wings and flowers onto the frosting and pipe on decorations with small gel icing tubes. Keep in an airtight container in a cool place for up to 3 days.

Silver Wedding Celebration Cupcakes

Makes 24

150 g/5 oz butter, softened
150 g/5 oz caster sugar
150 g/5 oz self-raising flour
25 g/1 oz ground almonds
3 medium eggs, beaten
1 tsp almond extract
2 tbsp milk

To decorate:
350 g/12 oz sugarpaste
edible silver dusting powder
450 g/1 lb fondant icing sugar
24 small silver ribbon bows

1. Preheat the oven to 180°C/350°F/Gas Mark 4. Line two 12-hole bun trays with silver foil cases.

2. Place the butter and sugar in a bowl, then sift in the flour and stir in the almonds. Add the beaten eggs to the bowl along with the almond extract and milk and beat until smooth. Spoon into the cases, filling them three-quarters full.

3. Bake for about 18 minutes until firm to the touch in the centre. Turn out onto a wire rack. Once cool, trim the tops of the cupcakes if they have peaked.

4. To decorate the cupcakes, first line an egg box with foil. Roll the sugarpaste into pea-sized balls and mould each one into a petal shape. Mould a cone shape and wrap a petal completely round this. Take another petal and wrap round the first, overlapping. Continue wrapping 4–5 petals round until a rose has formed. Pull the thick base away, flute out the petals and place in the egg box. Repeat until you have 24 roses. Leave them to dry out for 2–4 hours. When they are firm, brush edible silver dust lightly over each rose with a clean paintbrush.

5. Make up the fondant icing sugar with water, according to the packet instructions, to a thick spreading consistency. Spread over the top of each cupcake. Work quickly, as the icing will set. Press a rose into the icing, and place a thin silver bow, on each cupcake. Leave to set for 30 minutes. Keep in a cool place for up to 2 days. Remove the bows before eating.

Golden Wedding Celebration Cupcakes

Makes 24

125 g/4 oz self-raising flour	To decorate:
	125 g/4 oz buttercream
125 g/4 oz caster sugar	(see page 29)
125 g/4 oz soft tub margarine	icing sugar, for dusting
	700 g/1½ lb ready-to-roll sugarpaste
2 medium eggs, beaten	yellow paste food colouring
1 tsp lemon juice	thin gold ribbon, curled

1. Preheat the oven to 180°C/350°F/Gas Mark 4. Line two 12-hole bun trays with small gold foil cases.

2. Sift the flour into a bowl and stir together with the caster sugar. Add the margarine and eggs and beat together with the lemon juice for about 2 minutes until smooth.

3. Spoon into the cases and bake for 15–20 minutes until golden and firm to the touch. Turn out on a wire rack. When cool, trim the tops flat if they have peaked slightly.

4. To decorate, lightly coat the top of each cupcake with a little buttercream. Dust a clean flat surface with icing sugar. Roll out two thirds of the sugarpaste and stamp out circles 6 cm/2½ inches wide and place these on the buttercream to cover the top of each cupcake.

5. Colour one eighth of the sugarpaste a deep yellow and mould this into thin sausage shapes. Leave these to dry for about 2 hours until firm. Roll out the remaining white sugarpaste and mark out small squares 4 x 4 cm (¾ x ¾ inch). Wrap a square round a yellow centre to form a lily and press the ends together. Make up all the lilies and place on the cupcakes. Cut short thin strips of gold paper ribbon and pull along the blade of a pair of scissors to curl and place on the cakes. Keep for up to 3 days in an airtight container in a cool place. Remove the ribbons before eating.

Bluebird Cupcakes

Makes 12–14

150 g/5 oz butter, softened
150 g/5 oz caster sugar
150 g/5 oz self-raising flour
3 medium eggs, beaten
1 tsp lemon juice
1 tbsp milk

To decorate:
125 g/4 oz sugarpaste
blue paste food colouring
icing sugar, for dusting
1 batch cream cheese frosting
  (see page 29)
white gel icing tube

1. Preheat the oven to 180°C/350°F/Gas Mark 4. Line a
   12-hole muffin tray with 12–14 deep paper cases,
   depending on the depth of the holes.

2. Place the butter and sugar in a bowl, then sift in the flour.
   Add the eggs to the bowl with the lemon juice and milk
   and beat until smooth. Spoon into the cases, filling them
   three-quarters full.

3. Bake for about 18 minutes until firm to the touch in the
   centre. Turn out to cool on a wire rack.

4. To decorate the cupcakes, colour the sugarpaste blue.
   Dust a clean flat surface with icing sugar. Roll out the
   sugarpaste thinly and cut out bird wings in sets of two
   and one body per bird, then stamp out some daisy shapes
   with a fluted daisy cutter. Leave all these to dry out for
   30 minutes until firm enough to handle.

5. Swirl the frosting onto each cupcake. Press one bird's
   body and pair of wings, and some flowers, onto the
   frosting and pipe on decorations with the white gel
   icing tubes. Keep in an airtight container in a cool
   place for up to 3 days.

Easter Nest Cupcakes

Makes 12

125 g/4 oz soft tub margarine
125 g/4 oz golden caster sugar
150 g/5 oz self-raising flour
2 tbsp cocoa powder
2 medium eggs
1 tbsp golden syrup

To decorate:
1 batch buttercream (*see* page 29)
50 g/2 oz shredded wheat cereal
125 g/4 oz milk chocolate,
  broken into pieces
25 g/1 oz unsalted butter
chocolate mini eggs

1. Preheat the oven to 180°C/350°F/Gas Mark 4. Line a
   12-hole bun tray with paper cases.

2. Place the margarine and the sugar in a large bowl, then
   sift in the flour and cocoa powder. In another bowl, beat
   the eggs with the syrup, then add to the first bowl. Whisk
   together with an electric beater for 2 minutes, or by
   hand with a wooden spoon, until smooth.

3. Divide the mixture between the cases, filling them three-
   quarters full. Bake for about 15 minutes until they are
   springy to the touch in the centre. Turn out to cool on a
   wire rack.

4. To decorate, swirl the buttercream over the top of each
   cupcake. Break up the shredded wheat finely. Melt the
   chocolate with the butter, then stir in the shredded
   wheat and let cool slightly. Line a plate with clingfilm.
   Mould the mixture into tiny nest shapes with your
   fingers, then place them on the lined plate. Freeze for a
   few minutes to harden. Set a nest on top of each cupcake
   and fill with mini eggs. Keep for up to 2 days in a cool
   place in an airtight container.

Harvest Festival Cupcakes

Makes 12

175 g/6 oz self-raising
  wholemeal flour
1 tsp baking powder
½ tsp ground cinnamon
pinch salt
150 ml/¼ pint sunflower oil
150 g/5 oz soft light brown sugar
3 medium eggs, beaten
1 tsp vanilla extract
50 g/2 oz sultanas
225 g/8 oz carrots, peeled and
  finely grated

To decorate:
1 batch cream cheese
  frosting (*see* page 29)
paste food colourings
225 g/8 oz ready-to-
  roll sugarpaste

1. Preheat the oven to 180°C/350°F/Gas Mark 4. Lightly oil a deep 12-hole muffin tray or line with deep paper cases.

2. Sift the flour, baking powder, cinnamon and salt into a bowl, along with any bran from the sieve.

3. Add the oil, sugar, eggs, vanilla extract, sultanas and grated carrots. Beat until smooth and then spoon into the muffin tray. Bake for 20–25 minutes until risen and golden. Cool on a wire rack.

4. To decorate, colour the frosting pale green and smooth over the top of each cupcake. Colour the sugarpaste in small batches of orange, red, green and brown and mould into cabbages, carrots, potatoes and tomatoes. Press green sugarpaste through a garlic press to make green carrot leaves. Place the vegetables on top of each cupcake. Keep for up to 3 days in an airtight container in a cool place.

Halloween Cobweb Cupcakes

Makes 16–18

175 g/6 oz caster sugar
175 g/6 oz soft tub margarine
3 medium eggs, beaten
150 g/5 oz self-raising flour
1 tsp baking powder
25 g/1 oz cocoa powder

To decorate:
225 g/8 oz icing sugar, sifted
2 tbsp warm water
orange and black paste food colourings

1. Preheat the oven to 180°C/350°F/Gas Mark 4. Line two 12-hole bun trays with 16–18 paper or foil cases, depending on the depth of the holes.

2. Place the sugar, margarine and eggs in a bowl, then sift in the flour, baking powder and cocoa powder. Beat for 2 minutes, or until smooth.

3. Spoon the mixture into the paper cases and bake for 15–20 minutes until well risen and the tops spring back when lightly pressed. Transfer to a wire rack to cool, then trim the tops of the cupcakes flat if they have any peaks.

4. To decorate the cupcakes, gradually mix the icing sugar with enough warm water to give a coating consistency. Colour a little of the icing black and place in a small paper icing bag. Colour the remaining icing bright orange.

5. Work on one cupcake at a time. Spread orange icing over the top of the cupcake. Snip a small hole from the base of the icing bag, then pipe a black spiral on top of the wet orange icing. Use a wooden cocktail stick and pull this through the icing to give a cobweb effect. Repeat with all the cupcakes and leave to set for 1 hour. Keep for up to 2 days in an airtight container in a cool place.

Sparkly Snowflake Cupcakes

Makes 24

150 g/5 oz butter, softened
150 g/5 oz caster sugar
150 g/5 oz self-raising flour
25 g/1 oz ground almonds
3 medium eggs, beaten
1 tsp almond extract
1 tbsp milk

To decorate:
icing sugar, for dusting
350 g/12 oz sugarpaste
450 g/1 lb royal icing
  sugar
edible silver balls

1. Preheat the oven to 180°C/350°F/Gas Mark 4. Line two 12-hole bun trays with silver foil cases.

2. Place the butter and sugar in a bowl, then sift in the flour and stir in the almonds. Add the beaten eggs to the bowl with the almond extract and milk. Spoon into the cases, filling them three-quarters full.

3. Bake for about 18 minutes until firm to the touch in the centre. Turn out onto a wire rack. Once cool, trim the tops of the cupcakes if they have peaked.

4. To decorate the cupcakes, dust a clean flat surface with icing sugar. Roll the sugarpaste thinly and mark out a snowflake pattern. Cut round the shapes and leave them to dry flat on a sheet of nonstick baking parchment for 2 hours until firm.

5. Make up the royal icing according to the packet instructions to a soft icing that will form peaks. Swirl the icing onto the cupcakes and place a snowflake shape centrally on each cupcake. Decorate with silver balls and leave for 30 minutes to set. Keep for up to 2 days in an airtight container.

Festive Candy Cane Cupcakes

Makes 14–18

150 g/5 oz butter, softened
150 g/5 oz caster sugar
150 g/5 oz self-raising flour
25 g/1 oz ground almonds
3 medium eggs, beaten
1 tsp vanilla extract
2 tbsp milk

To decorate:
225 g/8 oz sugarpaste
red and green paste food colourings
icing sugar, for dusting
450 g/1 lb royal icing sugar

1. Preheat the oven to 180°C/350°F/Gas Mark 4. Line two 12-hole
   bun trays with 14–18 foil cases, depending on the depth of the holes.

2. Place the butter and sugar in a bowl, then sift in the flour and
   stir in the almonds. Add the eggs to the bowl along with the
   vanilla extract and milk. Spoon into the cases, filling them
   three-quarters full.

3. Bake for about 18 minutes until firm to the touch in the
   centre. Turn out onto a wire rack. Once cool, trim the tops of
   the cupcakes if they have peaked.

4. To decorate, colour one quarter of the sugarpaste red and one
   quarter green. Dust a clean flat surface with icing sugar. Roll out
   the sugarpaste into long, very thin sausages with the palms of
   your hands. Roll a sausage of red with a sausage of white to form
   a twist. Cut into short lengths about 5 cm/2½ inches long and
   bend round to form a cane shape. Repeat with green and white
   sugarpaste. Leave to dry out flat for 2 hours until firm.

5. Make up the royal icing according to the packet instructions
   to a soft icing that will form peaks. Smooth the icing onto
   the cupcakes and place a cane centrally on each one. Place the
   remaining icing in a small piping bag fitted with a star nozzle
   and pipe a star border round the outside of each cupcake.
   Keep for up to 2 days in an airtight container.

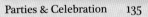

Hanukkah Honey Spice Cupcakes

Makes 12–14

1 tsp instant coffee granules
6 tbsp hot water
175 g/6 oz plain flour
1 tsp baking powder
½ tsp bicarbonate of soda
½ tsp ground cinnamon
½ tsp ground ginger
pinch ground cloves
2 medium eggs
125 g/4 oz golden caster sugar
175 g/6 oz honey
5 tbsp vegetable oil
50 g/2 oz walnuts, finely chopped
125 g/4 oz golden icing sugar, to decorate

1. Preheat the oven to 160°C/325°F/Gas Mark 3. Line one or two muffin trays with 12–14 deep paper cases, depending on the depth of the holes. Dissolve the coffee in the water and leave aside to cool.

2. Sift the flour with the baking powder, bicarbonate of soda and spices. In another bowl, beat the eggs with the sugar and honey until smooth and light, then gradually beat in the oil until blended. Stir this into the flour mixture along with the coffee and walnuts. Beat until smooth.

3. Carefully spoon the mixture into the paper cases. Fill each halfway up. Be careful not to overfill them, as the mixture will rise up. Bake for 25–30 minutes until they are risen, firm and golden. Leave in the trays for 5 minutes, then turn out onto a wire rack to cool.

4. To decorate, blend the icing sugar with 1 tbsp warm water to make a thin glacé icing. Place in a paper icing bag and snip away the tip. Pipe large daisies over each cupcake and leave to set for 30 minutes. Keep in an airtight container for up to 5 days.

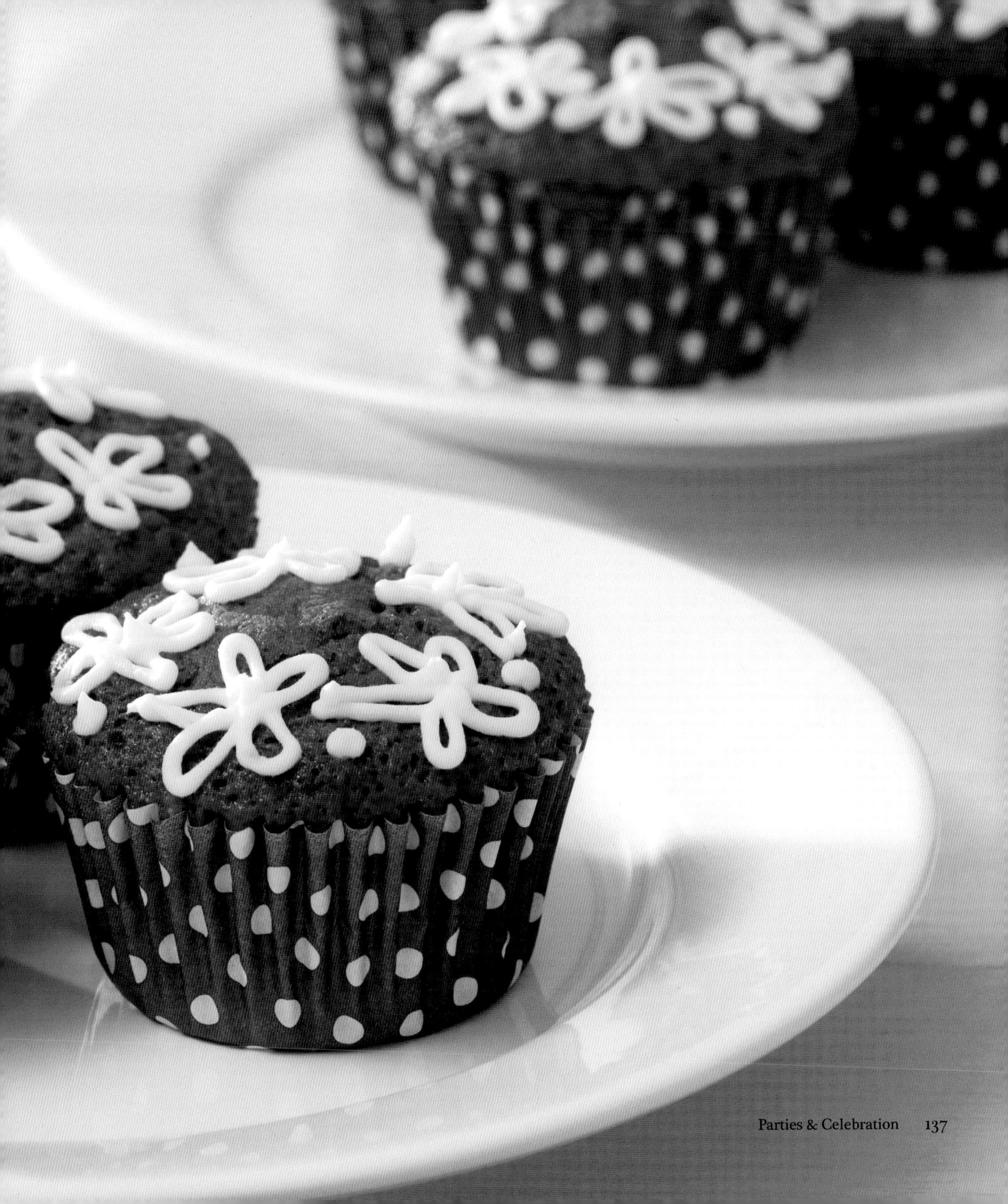

Giftwrapped Presents Cupcakes

Makes 12–14

125 g/4 oz butter
125 g/4 oz soft dark muscovado sugar
2 medium eggs, beaten
225 g/8 oz self-raising flour
1 tsp ground mixed spice
finely grated zest and 1 tbsp juice from 1 orange
1 tbsp black treacle
350 g/12 oz mixed dried fruit

To decorate:
3 tbsp sieved apricot glaze (*see* page 31)
icing sugar, for dusting
600 g/1 lb 5 oz ready-to-roll sugarpaste
red, blue, green and yellow paste food
  colourings

1. Preheat the oven to 180°C/350°F/Gas Mark 4. Line one or two 12-hole muffin trays with 12–14 deep paper cases, depending on the depth of the holes.

2. Beat the butter and sugar together until light and fluffy, then beat in the eggs a little at a time, adding 1 tsp flour with each addition. Sift in the remaining flour and spice, add the orange zest and juice, treacle and dried fruit to the bowl and fold together until the mixture is blended.

3. Spoon into the cases and bake for about 30 minutes until firm in the centre and a skewer comes out clean. Leave to cool in the trays for 15 minutes, then turn out to cool on a wire rack. Store undecorated in an airtight container for up to 4 weeks, or freeze until needed.

4. To decorate, trim the top of each cupcake level if they have peaked, then brush with apricot glaze. Dust a clean flat surface with icing sugar. Colour the sugarpaste in batches and roll out thinly. Cut out circles 6 cm/2½ inches wide. Place a disc on top of each cupcake and press level. Mould coloured scraps into long thin sausages and roll these out thinly. Place a contrasting colour across each cupcake and arrange into bows and loops. Leave to dry for 24 hours if possible. Keep for up to 4 days in an airtight container.

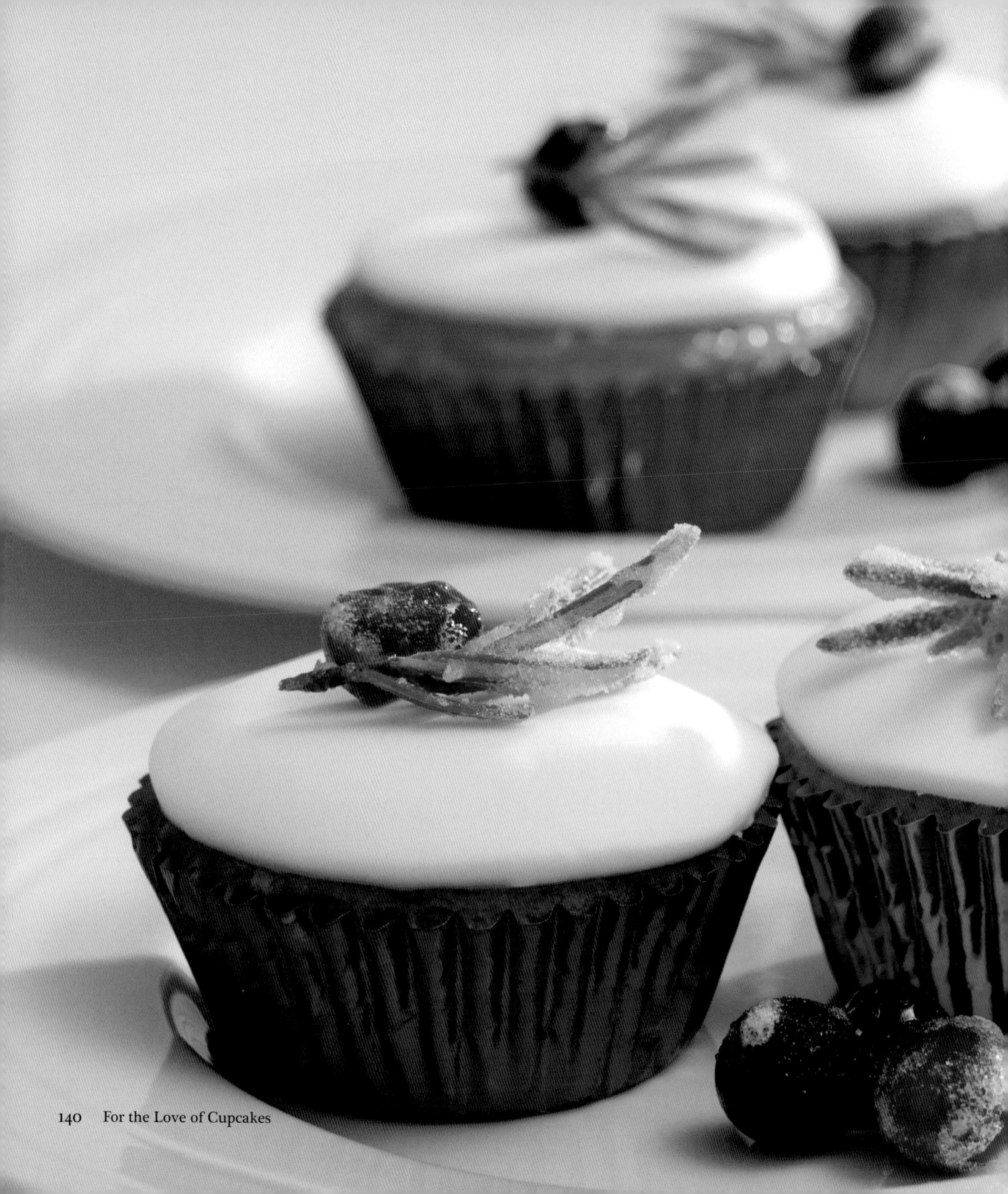

Crystallized Rosemary & Cranberry Cupcakes

Makes 12

125 g/4 oz self-raising
  flour
125 g/4 oz butter,
  softened
125 g/4 oz golden
  caster sugar
2 medium eggs, beaten
zest of ½ orange,
  finely grated

To decorate:
1 egg white
12 small rosemary sprigs
125 g/4 oz fresh red
  cranberries
caster sugar, for dusting
3 tbsp apricot glaze, sieved
  (*see* page 31)
icing sugar, for dusting
350 g/12 oz ready-to-roll
  sugarpaste

1. Preheat the oven to 180°C/350°F/Gas Mark 4. Line a
   12-hole bun tray with foil fairy cake cases.

2. Sift the flour into a bowl and add the butter, sugar, eggs
   and orange zest. Beat for about 2 minutes until smooth,
   then spoon into the paper cases.

3. Bake in the centre of the oven for about 14 minutes until
   well risen and springy in the centre. Transfer to a wire
   rack to cool.

4. To decorate, place a sheet of nonstick baking parchment
   on a flat surface. Beat the egg white until frothy, then
   brush thinly over the rosemary and cranberries and place
   them on the nonstick baking parchment. Dust with caster
   sugar and leave to dry out for 2–4 hours until crisp.

5. Brush the top of each fairy cake with a little apricot glaze.
   Dust a clean flat surface with icing sugar, roll out the
   sugarpaste and cut out 12 circles 6 cm/2½ inches wide.
   Place a disc on top of each and press level. Decorate each
   one with sparkly rosemary sprigs and cranberries. Keep
   for up to 3 days in an airtight container in a cool place.

White Chocolate Christmas Cupcakes

Makes 12–16

150 g/5 oz butter, softened
150 g/5 oz caster sugar
150 g/5 oz self-raising flour
3 medium eggs, beaten
1 tsp vanilla extract
1 tbsp milk
75 g/3 oz white chocolate,
  finely grated

To decorate:
250 g/9 oz white
  chocolate, chopped
16 holly leaves, cleaned
  and dried
1 batch buttercream
  (*see* page 29)
icing sugar, for dusting

1. Preheat the oven to 180°C/350°F/Gas Mark 4. Line one or two 12-hole bun trays with 12–16 foil cases, depending on the depth of the holes.

2. Place the butter and sugar in a bowl, then sift in the flour. Add the eggs to the bowl with the vanilla extract and milk and beat until smooth. Fold in the grated white chocolate, then spoon into the cases, filling them three-quarters full.

3. Bake for about 18 minutes until firm to the touch in the centre. Turn out to cool on a wire rack.

4. To decorate, melt the white chocolate in a heatproof bowl standing over a pan of barely simmering water. Use one third of the melted chocolate to paint the underside of the holly leaves and leave to set for 30 minutes in the refrigerator. Spread one third of the chocolate out onto a clean plastic board. When almost set, make into curls by pulling a sharp knife through the chocolate at an angle until the chocolate curls away from the knife. Stir the remaining cooled chocolate into the buttercream and chill for 15 minutes.

5. Swirl each cupcake with buttercream, then press on the white chocolate curls. Peel the holly leaves away from the chocolate and carefully place on top of the cupcakes. Dust with icing sugar before serving. Keep for up to 2 days in the refrigerator.

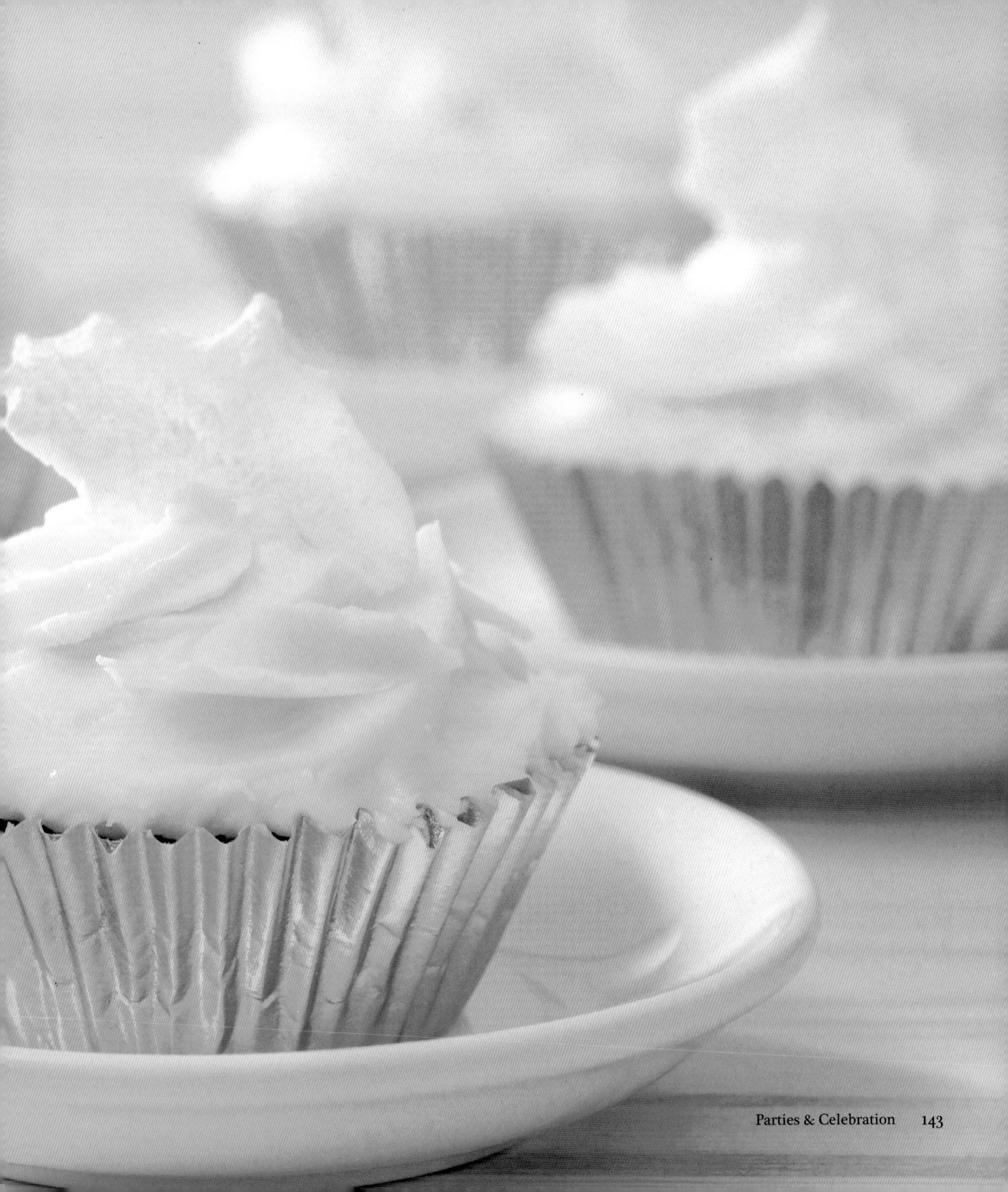

Index